ARE YOU BEING ABUSED?

ARE YOU BEING ABUSED?

BULLYING · ASSAULT · FEAR · NEGLECT · RAPE · ABUSE · MOLESTATION

Sherri
Mabry
Gordon

Enslow Publishing
101 W. 23rd Street
Suite 240
New York, NY 10011
USA

enslow.com

Acknowledgments

I would like to acknowledge and thank all those who contributed their stories and their experiences. For those who have suffered abuse, I admire your courage to share. Thank you for telling your stories. For those working to address the issue of abuse, I admire your hard work and determination. Thank you for all you do. —S.M.G.

Published in 2016 by Enslow Publishing, LLC
101 W. 23rd Street, Suite 240, New York, NY 10011

Library of Congress Cataloging-in-Publication Data

Gordon, Sherri Mabry.
 Are you being abused? / Sherri Mabry Gordon.
     pages cm. — (Got issues?)
 Includes bibliographical references and index.
 Summary: "Discusses problems and difficulties facing those who are being abused, including ways to help"—Provided by publisher.
 ISBN 978-0-7660-6979-4
 1. Child abuse—Juvenile literature. 2. Child sexual abuse—Juvenile literature. 3. Abused children—Juvenile literature. 4. Abused teenagers—Juvenile literature. 5. Sexually abused teenagers—Juvenile literature. I. Title.
 HV6626.5.G67 201
 362.76—dc23   2015011772

Printed in the United States of America

To Our Readers: We have done our best to make sure all Web site addresses in this book were active and appropriate when we went to press. However, the author and the publisher have no control over and assume no liability for the material available on those Web sites or on any Web sites they may link to. Any comments or suggestions can be sent by e-mail to customerservice@enslow.com.

Portions of this book originally appeared in the book *Beyond Bruises: The Truth About Teens and Abuse.*

Disclaimer: For many of the images in this book, the people photographed are models. The depictions do not imply actual situations or events.

Photo Credits: Aleksei Potov/Shutterstock.com, p. 23; bbevren/Shutterstock.com, p. 47; Courtesy of Nicole Braddock Bromley, p. 29; Federico Marsicano/Shutterstock.com, p. 7; bikeriderlondon/Shutterstock.com, pp. 75, 91; CREATISTA/Shutterstock.com, p. 81; Concept Photo/Shutterstock.com, p. 69; David TB/Shutterstock.com, p. 77; deeepblue/Shutterstock.com, p. 54; diplomedia/Shutterstock.com, p. 57; enciktat/Shutterstock.com, p. 101; frank_peters/Shutterstock.com, p. 51; Kamira/Shutterstock.com, p. 85; mangostock/Shutterstock.com, p. 94; mrkornflakes/Shutterstock.com, p. 89; National Center on Domestic and Sexual Violence, pp. 42, 62, 79; otnaydur/Shutterstock.com, p. 11; Photosani/Shutterstock.com, p. 26; Petrenko Andriy/Shutterstock.com, p. 18; Piotr Marcinski/Shutterstock.com, p. 3; Piotr Wawrzyniuk/Shutterstock.com, p. 66; Pixel Memoirs/Shuttestock.com, p. 60; Rob Marmion/Shutterstock.com, p. 97; SpeedKingz/Shutterstock.com, p. 37; threerocksimages/Shutterstock.com, p. 33.

Cover Credit: Piotr Marcinski/Shutterstock.com (depressed teen).

Author's Note

In this book, the author sometimes refers to domestic abuse and teen dating violence victims as girls and women and abusers as men and boys because research shows that 90 to 95 percent of all victims are female. This decision is not intended to downplay the seriousness of violence against males. Additionally, some of the names of those who shared their stories and experiences have been changed to protect their privacy.

Contents

Chapter 1 The Quest for Power and Control:
Understanding Abuse 7

Chapter 2 Houses of Pain:
Abuse Inside the Home 23

Chapter 3 Unhealthy Relationships:
Abuse Outside the Home 37

Chapter 4 The High Cost of Abuse:
How Teens Are Affected 57

Chapter 5 Abuse and the Community:
A Look at the Impact on Society 69

Chapter 6 Ending the Violence:
How to Help and Get Help 77

Chapter 7 What's Next? Addressing Abuse in
the Future 94

Chapter Notes 105

Glossary 117

For More Information 121

Further Reading 125

Index 126

The Quest for Power and Control: Understanding Abuse

What began as fairytale romance was anything but magical. In fact, it quickly became a nightmare for twenty-year-old Katie. While studying abroad in Milan, Italy, she met Matt, who appeared to be everything she was looking for in a boyfriend. The two quickly became inseparable.

"Dating him wasn't like dating the frat guys from college," Katie explains. "Plus, there's something romantic about falling in love in a foreign country. Every girl wants that kind of story."

Despite the allure of being in love and in another country, Katie's situation also made her vulnerable. She was halfway around the world and separated from friends and family. And the relationship was moving quickly.

"It went from being nothing to being something very quickly," she says. "It was very fast-paced. We went from zero to sixty very quickly."

Still, Matt's abusive behavior was not as noticeable while they were abroad. And even though she knew he had hit his previous girlfriend, she explained it away. So she continued the relationship.

"He told me he loved me within three to four weeks. He also told me he wanted to spend the rest of his life with me," she says. "But he also would look through my phone and accuse me of being a horrible person."

Once they returned to the United States, the emotional abuse escalated, and in the end, it became physical and life altering.

"When I returned from abroad, the next six months were the worst of my life," Katie says. "I lived off campus, so he would call or Skype and then threaten me if I left. He basically isolated me from my friends and family."

Katie says he also made her feel incapable of being loved and convinced her that she did not deserve friendships. He berated her, called her a whore, and told her she was a horrible person.

"I never left my apartment," she explains, "and I felt like I was incapable of being loved. It was getting to the point where I would cry every day from the moment I would wake up to the moment I would go to sleep."

Finally, Katie realized she needed to get out of the relationship. But Matt did not make it easy. He told her that she was destroying him and that he did not have a reason to live.

"The last time I saw him, he raped me," Katie says. "I have been in therapy ever since. He took a piece of me. I was a happy-go-lucky girl without a care in the world. And I turned into a hermit who was scared to be alone because of what he did to me."

Katie was afraid of him, and even though she blocked his number, he still found ways to contact her.

"He continued to contact me until he found a new person," she says.

Initially, Katie tried to ignore that she had been raped. She did not tell anyone what had happened to her. But it eventually came out.

"I couldn't admit that he raped me," she says.

Eventually Katie found the courage to tell her parents. And they encouraged her to seek counseling and start healing. Initially, Katie was not a huge proponent of therapy, but she admits that it has helped her tremendously.

"I have learned to put [what happened to me] in a box and not let it control my every day life," she says. "Now it's not always in the forefront of my life."

Today, Katie has graduated from college and is working in health care. She also continues with her therapy and focuses on taking care of herself, which includes everything from eating right, exercising, and meditating to attending church, hanging out with friends, and doing things she enjoys. She also hopes to share her story with other young women.

"Therapy has helped me see that I wasn't alone," she says. "At the time, I thought I was the only person who went through what I did. If I had had someone to talk to me [about abuse] then maybe I would have left the relationship sooner rather than later."

Currently, Katie is discussing options for speaking on behalf of the One Love Foundation. The One Love Foundation was created in 2010 following the death of Yeardley Love, a University of Virginia senior who lost her life at the hands of her ex-boyfriend.

"The biggest thing I want to tell young girls is to trust your instincts," she says. "If you get a bad feeling or a hint that something is not right, get out. Don't hope that you can change someone because you can't."[1]

How to Recognize Abuse

Abuse can take many different forms. It may be physical, sexual, emotional, verbal, or a combination of any of these. Teens can experience abuse in a number of different environments—at home, on a date, at school, at a friend or relative's house, at work, and even online.

For example, some children grow up in abusive homes where they witness violence between their parents. They might see their dad or their stepfather scream at their mom and maybe even slap, push, or hit her. This type of abuse among adult couples is often called domestic violence. Teens might experience abuse in a dating relationship or be sexually abused by a relative or a friend of the family. Others may be harassed or bullied at school or over the Internet.

Many people think abuse is about anger or sex, but it is really about power and control. When one person abuses another, it is because he or she wants to be the one in control. For example, someone who is abusive may want to make all the decisions for another person, including what that person can wear and who that person can spend time with. Other times abusers feel more powerful and in control when they make other people cry or feel bad about themselves. Often, abusers gain control in a relationship because they seem to have all the power. For example, they might be bigger and stronger or in a position of authority—which seems to imply they should have more power than the victim.

Abuse can affect anyone regardless of race, religion, or social standing. It does not matter how much money a family has or whether they live in the city, the suburbs, or out in the country. Every teen is susceptible to abuse. Therefore, it is important to know what constitutes abuse.

Physical Abuse

Physical abuse is often the most obvious form of abuse. It can include everything from hitting, pushing, slapping, shaking, pinching, biting, restraining, grabbing, and choking to beating, burning, whipping, kicking, and throwing a person. Essentially, physical abuse is any physical action that leaves marks or causes pain or injury.

Sexual Abuse and Assault

Any type of sexual contact between an adult and a child is sexual abuse. Sexual abuse can also exist in teen dating relationships. It can

Physical abuse is the most obvious form of abuse since it usually leaves visible marks that other people can see. Other types of abuse, however, can be just as painful.

even occur between children. For example, a child who is abused may act out the abuse on another child. Sometimes the child being victimized is younger, and sometimes he or she is simply more vulnerable. Nicole Braddock Bromley, an expert on childhood sexual abuse and founder of OneVOICE Enterprises, believes that sexual abuse is about exerting power over another in order to act out sexually.

Bromley says:

> *I don't think age should be the main focus (or factor). It is more about a perceived sense of power. I hear stories all the time about kids being in the same grade—like first grade—and being sexually abused by their classmate who sits right next to them. The details*

*of the story seldom lead me to think they are just experimenting.
When one child is acting out of power or control over the other,
the effects it has on the victim are the same as any other victim
of sexual abuse. So it makes me cringe when people say, "Well, it
wasn't really sexual abuse because they were the same age"—that
takes a lot away from the victim. The victim needs to know that
what happened was wrong and it wasn't their fault.*[2]

In general, sexual abuse involves words, looks, touches, or all three. It can be nonphysical, or it can be physical and even violent. These words, looks, and touches can include everything from commenting on a young person's developing body to exposing a child to pornography to inappropriate touching and sexual assault.

Sexual assault, which is sometimes called rape, is unwanted sex. It is a brutal form of sexual abuse and can involve physical force or coercion.

When young people are sexually abused or raped by a member of their family, this is called incest. Molestation is another name for sexual abuse and involves both physical contact, as well as interactions between a young person and an adult. It is also considered molestation when a teenager engages sexually with a child. Usually the molester is in a position of authority or power over the victim.

Another form of sexual abuse is sexual harassment, which often occurs at work, at school, or online. This type of abuse includes unwelcome sexual attention and it can happen both verbally or physically. For example, sexually harassing someone verbally might include telling a crude sexual joke or commenting on one of his or her body parts. Some examples of sexually harassing someone physically would be pushing up against him or her in a crowded hallway, grabbing another person's private parts, and touching another person and making it look like an accident. Sexual harassment may create a hostile or threatening atmosphere for the victim.

Verbal Abuse

People often think that verbal abuse is just name-calling, but it is actually more than that. Verbal abusers attempt to define another person with words. They also try to define a person's thoughts, feelings, and motives. For example, Patricia Evans, an expert on verbal abuse, says:

Verbal abusers tell you:

Who you are: "You are the teacher's pet."

What you are: "You are a wimp."

How you are: "You are too sensitive."

How you feel: "You've got nothing to cry about."

What you are trying to do: "You are just trying to get attention."

What your future will be: "You will never amount to anything."

What you want: "You want everything your way."

What to do: "Just get over it."

While not all verbal abuse will lead to violence, it often precedes it. Usually teens who become violent will express their anger in revealing words and comments before the violence erupts.[3]

Emotional Abuse

Emotional abuse can be the most difficult form of abuse to detect because it is often subtle. This type of abuse includes both verbal attacks and the withholding of emotional support and approval. Victims of emotional abuse are rarely complimented or told what they do well. Instead, they are criticized, humiliated, and intimidated on a regular basis. They are also "hit" with words and statements that are hurtful, blaming, rejecting, critical, or sarcastic in nature. Someone who is emotionally abusive may also try to isolate the person from family and friends.

Emotional abuse is confusing for young people because it usually comes from someone who claims to care about them. They hear two messages; one says, "I love you," while the other says, "Who you are is not okay." This type of treatment causes people to feel worthless. They cannot believe that someone who cares about them would say something that is not true. A majority of those who have been abused say that emotional abuse is harder to endure than physical abuse.[4]

Additional Types of Abuse

There are several other types of abuse that children and teens can be exposed to. These types of abuse include neglect, bullying, stalking, exploitation and trafficking, and cyberbullying. These forms of abuse may include a combination of physical, verbal, emotional, and sexual abuse.

Neglect. Children or teens are considered neglected when their parents or caregivers do not provide food, housing, clothing, medical care, or supervision. Young people also can be neglected emotionally. This happens when a parent does not provide enough emotional support or when they pay little to no attention to the child.

Bullying. People bully other people by intimidating them. Most often bullying occurs among peers or people who are close in age. Bullies use threats and humiliation to get others to do what they want. They may even use physical force, such as pushing or shoving. There are six types of bullying. These include physical bullying, verbal bullying, relational aggression, cyberbullying, sexual bullying, and prejudicial bullying.

Cyberbullying. When a young person uses the Internet or technology to harass, threaten, embarrass, or target another person, this is called cyberbullying. Typically, cyberbullying involves teens and is through social media, text messaging, FaceTime, and other popular communication methods. If an adult is involved, this is considered cyberstalking or cyber-harassment. People cyberbully others by harassing them, impersonating them, creating websites, or blogs about them, and using photos and videos to humiliate or embarrass them.

Stalking. Stalking generally involves harassing or threatening behavior that happens repeatedly over a period of time. This

A Closer Look

Emotional abuse is subtle and often hard to detect. Unlike physical abuse, there are no visible marks. The words and actions can be masked in what seem to be normal words or behavior. In fact, victims of emotional abuse often do not realize that they are being abused—they just know that they feel bad about themselves. They know there is something about what was said or done that just does not "feel right," but they often have a hard time communicating it to other people.

To accurately describe emotional abuse to another person, the victim needs to describe more than just the words being said. He or she also needs to describe the abuser's tone of voice (sarcastic), attitude (disdain or contempt), gestures (pointing a finger), and stance (towering over the victim).

The Helping Teens Web site has compiled an overview of the various aspects of emotional abuse. These are listed below.

Rejecting—Not acknowledging someone's "presence, value or worth"; communicating that the person is worthless; telling a person that his or her thoughts and feelings do not matter or that they are wrong

Degrading—Insulting, ridiculing, name calling, imitating. . . publicly humiliating or labeling a person as stupid

Terrorizing—Causing terror or extreme fear; intimidating a person; making threats; exposing a person to something scary

Isolating—Putting limits on personal contact with others; limiting freedom to make decisions; denying access to money or medical attention

Corrupting/Exploiting—Convincing someone to do something against the law; using a person to make money; training someone to meet the needs of the abuser only

Denying Emotional Responsiveness—Being detached and uninvolved (sometimes called "emotionally unavailable"); interacting only when necessary; failing to show affection.[5]

behavior can include following a person, appearing at a person's home, threatening a person, making harassing phone calls, leaving written messages, and vandalizing property. Cyberstalking occurs online and shares many characteristics with physical stalking. Even though cyberstalking does not involve physical contact, that does not mean it is less harmful or scary. In fact, online harassment and threats may lead to more serious behavior, such as physical violence.

Exploitation and trafficking. Exploitation and trafficking are two other forms of abuse. Exploitation, which is sometimes called commercial sexual exploitation of children (CSEC), is a form of sexual abuse and involves a cash payment to the child or to a third party, such as a parent. The child is treated as a commercial and sexual object. CSEC can involve prostitution and pornography, as well as the sale and trafficking of children for other sexual purposes.

Trafficking involves moving people from one place to another for the purpose of sex, slavery, or forced labor. The trafficking of young people involves a series of events: acquiring the children or teens, moving them, and exploiting them. To do this, the abusers may use force, tricks, or drugs. For example, young people from impoverished areas are sometimes lured from their homes with promises of a job in another country. They go along because they want to help their family. But once they arrive in the new country, there is no job. Instead, they are often beaten, threatened with death if they try to escape, and forced into prostitution.

Sometimes the family knows about the trafficking and agrees to it as a way to make money, and sometimes the young person initiates it. Other times, young people are taken against their will and without their family's knowledge.

Pattern of Abuse

Abuse is not a one-time act. There is a pattern to the behavior. It is both repeated and sustained. Typically, abuse follows a cycle with three, or sometimes four, phases.

(1) tension-building phase

(2) incident phase

(3) make-up phase (not always part of the cycle)

(4) calm phase

Understanding these phases of abuse is important not only for victims of abuse but also for those helping them. People can use the phases to determine another person's risk for injury when trying to help.

Tension-building phase. In the tension-building phase, victims of abuse can feel the frustration of their abuser. They have a sense that something is going to happen soon, and they start to get fearful. Experts say people who suffer abuse for a long time can often predict when it is going to happen. They know the signs of abuse and may watch for them.

During the tension-building phase, victims will sometimes do what they can to keep the abuser happy. Children might try really hard to be good. Or a teen girl with an abusive boyfriend might try to please him. An abused wife might try to stay out of the way or avoid doing anything that would anger her husband. Victims often feel as if they are walking on eggshells during this phase.

By doing the "right" things, victims may hope they can keep the abuse from happening. However, they are powerless to do so. No one can control another person. People make their own choices. People victimized by abuse will never be able to change their abusers by doing something better or by being different. Nor will they be able to love their abusers enough to change them.

Incident phase. The incident phase may consist of just one incident, or it may include several incidents throughout the day or over a period of days or months. It normally involves an escalation of the abuse, which means the abuse increases in intensity and severity. It may grow from occasional put-downs to screaming, throwing things, and breaking objects or to pushing, shoving, and hitting. The abuse in this phase may be physical, verbal, emotional, or sexual. Or it may include several types of abuse.

In the tension-building phase, victims do their best to prevent an incident from happening. The stress of walking on eggshells and trying to please the abuser can wear on them.

For example, an abusive parent might scream at her child, call him stupid for forgetting to take the trash out, and then make him sit in the trash can for an hour. An abusive boyfriend might call his girlfriend names, curse at her, tell her that no one would ever want her, and then refuse to speak to her for a few days. An abusive husband might yell at his wife for spending ten dollars at the store and shove the checkbook in her face, which knocks her to the floor. The incident phase may consist of just one incident, or it may include several incidents throughout the day or over a period of days or months.

Make-up phase. Sometimes abusive people will feel sorry for their actions. When an abuser apologizes, the abuse moves into what is called the make-up phase. During this phase, abusers might even purchase gifts or give flowers. They may promise that it will never happen again. These things are often just another way to control the victim. The abuser is apologizing to keep the person being abused from breaking up or telling someone. But the behavior does not change. Not all abusers will say they are sorry and attempt to make up. Therefore, this phase only exists in some cases.

Many times abusers make excuses for their behavior, or they try to convince the victim that the abuse was not as bad as he or she claims or that it is a normal aspect of the relationship. They may even blame the victim or deny that abuse occurred. These tactics are called minimizing, blaming, and denying, and they are considered emotionally abusive. These actions are also controlling and can confuse the person victimized by abuse.

Calm phase. The final phase of the abuse cycle is the calm phase. During this phase, the people involved behave as if the incident has been forgotten. Very little abuse, if any, takes place. Things appear normal, and the people victimized by abuse often hope that the abuse will not happen again. They may also feel loved in this phase, which may make them wonder if the abuse was as bad as they remember.

Grooming. With sexual abuse, there is another important element known as grooming. It is the method that a sex offender uses to make a child more accepting of his advances. In other words, he is preparing the child for what he has planned in the future. Grooming builds trust and makes the child feel comfortable. It is important to note that sexual abuse does not usually start out as rape. Instead, the sexual abuse happens little by little. For example, the first phase in the grooming process might include watching pornographic movies together. Later, the offender may move to looks and touches and maybe even to sexual assault.

Time span. Because every situation is different, there is no set amount of time that each phase lasts. Nor is there a set amount of time for abuse to make a complete cycle through the phases. For example, it can take just a few hours to more than a year to complete the cycle. Verbal and emotional abuse may be present in every phase of the cycle.

Typically, unless people get help, abuse is ongoing. The cycle keeps repeating itself. With time, abuse may happen more often and get worse. This often makes people being victimized feel powerless to stop the abuse. They may feel they deserve to be treated poorly, and they may feel bad about themselves. Sometimes later in life, these same children and teens, especially boys, can become abusers themselves without treatment. When this happens, they are often trying to gain the control they never had as children. The only way to stop the cycle of abuse is if both the victims and the abusers get help. They need to learn what healthy relationships look like.

What Motivates an Abuser?

Aside from the basic need for power and control, there are a number of reasons why someone might choose to abuse another person. Sometimes abuse comes from a sense of entitlement, which happens when people feel like something is owed to them. When entitlement is the root, the abusers are usually males who believe that it is their right to have ultimate authority over a female in a relationship.

Sometimes entitlement means they think everything will always go their way. They have not been told "no" very much growing up, and they have not learned how to compromise in a relationship. When things do not go their way, they get frustrated and mad. They try to control the other person so they can get their way and be in charge.

Pornography can also play a role when it comes to abuse. For example, repetitive use of pornography and sexual fantasy sometimes desensitizes a person and causes him or her to have a distorted view of people and of sex. For instance, adult pornography often causes male users to see women as objects to be controlled and used. In some cases, the person will act out his or her sexual fantasies with the victim. At other times, the offender will use pornography as a tool in abusing another person sexually. In fact, a number of sexual offenders report also having an addiction to pornography and using it to abuse another.

"In about 90 percent of the stories I hear from people across the country, their abusers used pornography or were involved in pornography," Nicole Braddock Bromley says.[6]

Sometimes growing up in an abusive home teaches people that abuse is a way of life. They may begin to believe that yelling, belittling, and hitting are what people do to each other. Alcohol and drugs can also play a role in abuse because alcohol and drugs impair people's ability to manage their behavior appropriately. Regular alcohol and drug abuse make it hard for a person to control their own life, so sometimes they try to control someone else's—usually the person closest to them. Fortunately, some people who grow up in abusive families realize that abuse is not acceptable. In addition, not everyone with a substance problem or a pornography addiction is abusive.

Ultimately, people who abuse others have a choice to make. Either they will continue to be abusive, or they will get help and learn how to make better choices when relating with others. With help, they can learn to relate in nonabusive ways. In the meantime, the important thing for victims to remember is that abuse is about the person doing it. It is not the victim's fault. And he or she does not have to endure it for the sake of the relationship or the family.

2

Houses of Pain:
Abuse in the Home

Daily spankings were a regular occurrence for Paige growing up. But these spankings were not what you might expect. Instead, she was left with bruises that stretched from the backs of her knees to her shoulder blades.

"God, please only allow one spanking today," Paige pleaded silently each morning, but she always got more than one beating. Paige was punished for everything from spilling a glass of milk at the breakfast table to not getting her chores done to not finishing her dinner.

"I remember trying to choose between being spanked and throwing up my dinner," says Paige.

Her mother used a thick ruler to punish Paige and her three siblings. She would pull their pants down and their shirts up and beat them. Even when they begged their mother to stop, the beatings always lasted a little longer. That's what Harold, the family's pastor, said parents should do.

"Harold taught the families in our church to begin spanking their children at six months of age," Paige recalls. "His theory was a lot like shock therapy. He thought if you spanked your child for being clumsy, then the child would no longer be clumsy. He also told parents to continue the spankings until the kids were begging for it to stop and then continue it a little longer [to make sure they learned their lesson]."

When the beating was finished, Paige's mother usually gave her a phrase to say, such as "I am a very disrespectful child" or "I am a disobedient child."[1]

Child Abuse

What Paige experienced growing up is called child abuse. Her mother physically abused her with the daily beatings, and she emotionally abused her by making Paige say negative things about herself. As Paige got older, the abuse did not end. It simply changed from being physical in nature to verbal and emotional abuse.

In general, child abuse is any behavior (physical, verbal, emotional, or sexual) that endangers or hurts a child physically or emotionally. The behavior can be directed at a child by a parent, stepparent, caregiver, or relative.

Sometimes people confuse discipline and abuse. But there are some big differences between the two. Discipline helps children learn to make good choices. Being disciplined for making poor choices helps teach children what appropriate behavior looks like. When young people are disciplined, they might feel angry or frustrated, but the discipline should not hurt them or make them feel bad about who they are. Some examples of discipline include losing privileges and being grounded.

Punishment does not involve teaching or instruction. It is about reacting to poor behavior and discouraging behavior by making the person hurt or feel bad. Punishment that is both extreme and harmful in some way is called abuse. Some examples of abuse include beating a child with an object such as a stick or a belt, slapping a child, locking a child in a closet, tying a child to a chair, or repeatedly calling the child names such as stupid, fat slob, idiot, or good-for-nothing.

For years, Paige kept silent about the punishment she received in her home. She was too scared to say anything. Her parents told her that if she talked about it, child protective services would take her away.

But one night at a friend's house, Paige talked about her mother's treatment of her. This led the family she was staying with to investigate the issue. Not long after her confession, the physical abuse in Paige's life stopped. But the verbal abuse remained constant.

Her mother called her names, blamed her for things, and put her down almost daily. She also expected Paige to keep her three younger siblings in line. When she was unable to do that, her mother became angry and ridiculed her.

Abuse is unfair to kids and can be extremely damaging. Young people have a hard time growing up healthy when they are abused. Kids should never be blamed for the abuse they suffer. It is not their fault. It is important for young people who are being abused to talk about what is happening with someone they trust, such as another relative, a teacher, a school counselor, a family friend, or a pastor.

Self-Abuse

Belinda was thirteen years old when she first cut her skin. The cuts were not deep, but the pain that caused it was. "There is a weird sense of calmness in it, that it makes you actually feel something," she says. Eventually, Belinda attempted suicide. While in the hospital, she received counseling to help her overcome self-injury. "Every once in a while, the thought would come back to do it, but I learned to do something else instead."[2]

Like Belinda, many teenagers who suffer from abuse cut or injure themselves. Professionals label this cutting as self-harm, self-injury,

Is Spanking Abuse?

In the United States, there is a growing controversy over whether or not spanking children should be considered abusive. Some argue that spanking opens the door to child abuse, while others believe that spanking can be a useful discipline tool when combined with other disciplinary actions (such as time-outs) and not used exclusively.

To complicate matters, there is research to support each side of the debate. For example, one study found that mothers who combined reasoning with negative consequences, such as spanking, had the most success in changing negative behaviors. Conversely, opponents argue that spanking hurts the parent-child relationship by making children feel less attached to their parents and less trusting of them.[3]

Currently, all fifty states permit parents to spank their children. However, twenty-nine states have laws that prohibit teachers from spanking or paddling students. Yet experts in raising children feel that eventually the country will ban spanking much like other countries have done.

In fact, a nurse in Massachusetts wrote a law in 2007 that would ban spanking in the state. She is hoping that the state will become the first in the nation to ban corporal punishment at home.

"I think it's ironic that domestic violence applies to everyone except the most vulnerable—children," says Kathleen Wolf, the nurse who wrote the bill.

Meanwhile, opponents of the bill argue that the government is trying to tell them how to parent their children. They feel the state is trying to take away what's been a tried-and-true method of child rearing.[4]

or self-inflicted violence. People might hurt themselves because they are depressed, anxious, or cannot cope with feelings. They may also feel worthless or unloved. But the majority of those who self-harm have been victimized by physical or sexual abuse.

According to the American Academy of Child and Adolescent Psychiatry (AACAP), teens that have trouble talking about their feelings may use self-harm as a way to express emotional pain and physical discomfort.[5]

Sexual Abuse

On the outside, Nicole Braddock looked like the perfect girl from the perfect family. She was the captain of three sports, homecoming queen, and president of the student council. Her family was well respected in the community. From the outside, Nicole's life seemed ideal.

But behind her cheery smile, straight A's, and bright eyes lurked a secret that filled her with shame, guilt, and confusion. Her stepfather had sexually abused her for almost a decade. During that time, he exposed her to pornography, touched her inappropriately, forced her to touch him, exposed himself, and sometimes made her take her clothes off. Yet Nicole kept silent. She struggled to find her voice and tell the secret—to seek help for the abuse she was enduring and the pain she was experiencing. Instead, fear kept her silent for years. Nicole explains:

> *I was afraid of breaking apart my family. I felt responsible for holding my family together. [My stepfather] always told me that if I told anyone that I would have to live with another family—that no one would believe me because I was just a little girl, and everyone would believe him. Of course I believed that. I also felt a lot of shame. I felt like it was my fault, and I didn't want other people to look at me differently or think I was disgusting.*

But finally, when Nicole was fourteen, she found the courage to tell her mother. After hearing her story, her mother reassured her that she would take care of it somehow. Several days later, her mother took action. She packed up Nicole, and they left their home. Nicole's mother reported the abuse to the local children's services organization. Soon an investigation was in process. Investigators talked separately with Nicole, her mother, and her stepfather—who denied everything. They were scheduled to appear in court the first day of Nicole's freshman year of high school.

Nicole says:

> *It was a big deal that my mom believed me. A lot of young people I talk with today are not believed or they are told not to talk about it. Unfortunately, that is more common than my situation. I feel very blessed that my mom believed me, did what was right in reporting it, took me out of the home, and protected me through the legal issues.*

While the investigation took place, Nicole and her mother tried to hide from her stepfather. They stayed with family and friends. A week after Nicole broke the silence, her stepfather committed suicide. Following her stepfather's death, the courts closed the case listing the abuse charges as substantiated. What this meant was that his suicide proved his guilt.

Nicole says:

> *Immediately I felt a lot of guilt [over his death]. My stepfather wasn't someone I hated. He was like two different people to me, and I felt like I had lost the father figure in my life. I also felt responsible for his death because I knew if I had kept this secret he would still be alive. I carried a lot of guilt for that. I also mourned his death because of the good side of him. That was very confusing for me because I'm thinking, "Well, this guy did these horrible things for many years, yet still I miss that other piece of him."*

After sharing her story with her mother, Nicole thought she could just put it all behind her. But as time went by, she realized she needed to talk about what had happened and she sought help. By

Nicole Braddock Bromley suffered for nearly a decade before she found the courage to admit that her stepfather was abusing her. She has made it her mission to help other victims speak out.

the time she was fifteen, Nicole shared her story publicly for the first time at a summer camp.

She recalls:

> *I told my story not knowing that anyone else there had ever experienced sexual abuse. Then when I got home, all these letters from other kids came pouring in telling me they had gone through the same thing and had never told anyone. That was an eye opener for me—that people needed a voice. Other kids needed to know that they were not alone. They needed someone to say, "It happened to me," so that they could say, "Me too."*

Today Nicole (now Nicole Braddock Bromley) says that as she looks back on her healing journey, she is glad she told the secret.

"I really believe the first step to healing is breaking the silence," she says.

As a result, Nicole is trying to help other young people find the courage to speak out about their abuse. She travels around the country to schools, universities, churches, and conferences educating others about childhood sexual abuse. She also founded OneVOICE enterprises, an organization whose purpose is to give a voice to those who have been victimized by sexual abuse.[6]

A Closer Look at Childhood Sexual Abuse

Like many children who are victimized sexually, Nicole knew her abuser and had a relationship with him. He was also in a position of authority. Most of the time if the abuser is bigger, older, or more powerful, victims cooperate because they are afraid of what will happen if they do not. In fact, in 95 percent of sexual abuse cases, victims know their abusers.[7]

The type of sexual abuse Nicole experienced is sometimes called incest. Incest consists of sexual interactions between family members, such as a father and a daughter, a father and a son, a mother and a son, a brother and a sister, or two brothers. Incest can also include sexual contact or interactions between a young person and another adult living in the home, such as a grandfather, an aunt, or an uncle. What sets incest apart from other forms of sexual abuse is that it takes place in the home.

As one researcher describes it, "[Incest] is a violation of the child where he or she lives. . . . A child molested by a stranger can run home for help and comfort. A victim of incest cannot."[8]

For this reason, experts believe sexual abuse in the home is one of the most underreported and least talked about abuses in the country. Threats from the abuser and pressure from other family members often keep abuse victims from getting help.

Sometimes victims do not seek help because they do not realize that what is happening is wrong. Often young victims believe the abuser who says it is a learning experience and that it happens in every family. They may even believe it is normal. Fear of being blamed or punished or that people will not believe them also keeps children silent.[9]

Nicole says that as a child she struggled with knowing whether or not what her stepfather was doing was wrong. She explains:

> For me it was, "Well, I guess it is normal." He would tell me that he was teaching me—that this is what "good dads do for their special daughters." It also happened little by little. [For example,] he would show me a pornographic video but not touch me. This video was his teaching tool—so in a sense he was grooming me for the actual touching or molestation that came later. Sexual abuse often begins slow and small like this, which creates a lot of confusion and questioning in the mind of a child.[10]

Another confusing aspect for childhood sexual abuse victims are the feelings associated with the abuse. For example, it can be confusing for a child when a touch that they believe is wrong can also feel good at the same time.

Bromley says:

> No one really talks about this aspect much, but when I talk about it at schools, the lightbulb turns on for people. If someone touches you or shows physical attention to your body, your body is going to respond to that. That is how your body is made. But I think [that response] causes a lot of shame.

> To personalize it, I thought I must be the most horrible disgusting person on this planet if it felt good when my stepfather touched me. How could I have felt that? For a long time, I believed that I had chosen that. But then I learned that I wasn't choosing it— that is just how our bodies are made. They are made to respond to touch. I wasn't making a choice—he was making the choice. Realizing that was really freeing for me.[11]

Statistics vary, but experts agree that sexual abuse is severely underreported. Still, it is estimated that one in seven boys are sexually abused by age sixteen, and one in three girls are sexually abused by age eighteen.[12]

It can deeply scar a young person who never talks about it. Without counseling or treatment, it creates a deep pain inside that never seems to go away.

Domestic Abuse

There is another type of abuse that can affect kids in the home. This type of abuse is sometimes called domestic violence, domestic abuse, or intimate partner violence. Domestic violence happens when one person in a relationship uses physical, emotional, verbal, or sexual abuse to control the other. The partners do not have to be married for the abuse to be considered domestic violence. When domestic abuse is present in a home, life is hard for the children.

Take Christy's home life as an example. Her home was filled with violence. When she was seven years old, her father took her and her siblings away from her mother. She did not see her mother again until she was fourteen. Her mother remarried her father in order to get her children back.

For the seven years Christy was separated from her mother, she watched her father abuse alcohol, date lots of women, and abuse her stepmother. And when her father was gone, her stepmother abused her and her siblings.

"[One time Daddy] was having a fight with my stepmother and he put all of us kids in the car . . . and he tried to run her over," Christy recalls. "She was running around the yard. . . . She would go hide by the tree and he would drive really close to the tree . . . really fast. [I remember being scared and thinking,] 'He's gonna kill her!'"[13]

Domestic violence, such as what Christy witnessed, is a big problem in the United States. In fact, one nationwide study found that one in four women has been abused by a husband or boyfriend.[14] Meanwhile, others report that as many as one in three women has been abused.[15] Overall, some experts believe that abuse

Domestic abuse doesn't only affect the partner being abused. Children who live in a home where domestic abuse is present suffer, as well. Many are abused themselves or develop emotional problems.

is hard to measure. Fear and shame keep many people who have been abused from making a report at all.[16]

Hundreds of studies have been done to determine the effects of domestic violence on children. The most obvious risk is that they, too, will become victims of abuse. In fact, studies show that in 30 to 60 percent of families affected by domestic violence, the children are also abused.[17] Even if children are not directly abused, they are still at risk for injury. Those at greatest risk are young children and teens. Young children get hurt because they cannot get out of the way. Meanwhile, teens put themselves at risk because they are more likely to try to stop the violence.

Young people who simply witness violence and abuse are also affected. They may experience any number of problems including being aggressive, depressed, fearful, anxious, stressed out, and so on.

Even if children never see the violence take place, they see the results. They might see bruises, holes in the walls, or broken furniture. Or they might wake up to yelling or screaming. They can sense the tension, which makes it hard for them to feel safe at home. Even if they feel physically safe, they often do not feel safe emotionally.

Consequences of Abuse

As many as 15.5 million US children live in families where domestic abuse occurred at least once in the past year. And 7 million children live in families with severe partner violence. This type of exposure takes its toll. Those who witness abuse at home often display similar symptoms to those who experience abuse.[18]

Here are some of the possible characteristics of children who have been exposed to domestic abuse:

- May be aggressive toward siblings or the nonabusive parent in ways that imitate the abusive parent
- May be overly compliant, accommodating, or try to please everyone
- May have low self-esteem
- May have poor health or complain of headaches, stomachaches, etc.
- May have poor impulse control or, conversely, may appear overly controlled
- May have academic problems or, conversely, may be an overachiever
- May be injured during violent incidents in the home
- May be abducted by the abuser or by the nonabusive parent to get them away from the abuse
- May be fearful or distrusting of close relationships[19]

Is Domestic Abuse also Child Abuse?

Sometimes when there is domestic abuse in a home, there is also child abuse but not always. Some experts have asked if simply being exposed to domestic abuse should be considered child abuse in the eyes of the law. But this is controversial.

Most states have laws that require doctors, school nurses, clergy (rabbis, pastors, priests, etc.), teachers, and others to file a report with child protective services anytime they suspect abuse in the home, regardless of whether the child has been directly abused. In other states, a report is not required. In these states, lawmakers believe that every case is different. Those required to make reports of abuse are permitted to assess each case individually.

Some experts believe that requiring a report in all cases is an example of a well-intentioned idea that has a negative effect. They note that in some domestic abuse cases, the children are not in immediate physical danger because the victim, usually the mother, has planned for their safety. Additionally, she is responding to their emotional needs.

Experts argue that a policy that defines child exposure to violence as neglect or abuse may be inaccurate and unfair to the victim. It implies that somehow the victim could have stopped the abuse.

In addition, involving child protective services may result in kids being removed from their mother. Separation from a parent may be worse for the kids than living in an abusive home may be. And if a victim believes that her kids will be taken away, she might be less likely to seek help. It may also discourage doctors and other professionals from reporting domestic abuse because they do not want to involve child protective services in their patient's life. Essentially, they argue that such a policy would only increase the silence surrounding domestic abuse.[20]

Instead, experts recommend placing nonabusive parents at the center of the decision making when it comes to their children. Doing so will empower them to make choices that enhance safety for them and for their children. This will also help restore healthy, nurturing environments in which young people can survive.

- May be homeless, as 28 percent of families who were homeless in 2008 were living on the streets because of domestic abuse[21]

Unhealthy Habits

Young people who grow up in homes where they are abused physically, emotionally, or sexually or witness abuse sometimes develop unhealthy habits. For example, they may:

Learn to keep secrets. They may be told not to tell anyone what happens at home. Or they may feel afraid to talk about it for fear of being hurt or being taken away. "This is a family matter" or "no one will believe you" are the messages they hear.

Learn that abuse is normal. Young people may believe that the way their family interacts is normal.

Learn not to trust people. Young people may grow up believing that they will be hurt by those who claim to love them. As a result, they may build a wall of self-protection.

Learn to take on more responsibility than they can handle. Many times, young people work hard to keep the peace, pacify the abuser, and stop the abuse. They may also feel guilty and blame themselves for the abuse in their homes. They believe the lie that if only they were better children, there would be no abuse.[22]

Unhealthy Relationships: Abuse Outside the Home

E veryone deserves a healthy relationship filled with respect, compassion, and equality. Yet many young people find themselves trapped in painful and abusive situations where they are so paralyzed with fear they cannot get out without help. While some do eventually leave and find freedom, there are those who never escape.

Take Jenny Crompton as an example. Jenny was a bright, articulate fourteen-year-old girl with a promising future. So it was no surprise that just a few months after starting high school, Jenny had a boyfriend.

She began dating Mark Smith, a tall, handsome senior. Her friends considered them the ideal couple because they shared a locker, ate lunch together, and walked each other to class. Even when Mark began to slap and shove Jenny and call her a slut, her friends thought it was no big deal—"that's just the way guys are."

Jenny tried to break up with Mark, but he ignored her. He refused to move out of her locker. He also continued to walk her to class and to call her. She got firmer. He got more possessive. Eventually, she gave up, and they got back together.

Finally, eleven months after their relationship started, Jenny cut ties with Mark again. This time it was for good. But Mark refused to go away. He burglarized her locker, broke into her home, and stalked her. He warned other boys to stay away from her, and he sent threatening notes. "You'll never make it to homecoming," he told her.

On homecoming day, Jenny got off the school bus and walked into her house. Mark was there waiting for her. He stabbed her more than sixty times with a butcher knife and left her lying in a pool of blood. Jenny was dead at age fifteen.[1]

"I was so high on adrenaline that there was no way that I could stop what I was doing until I came down from that rush," says Smith, describing the day he stabbed Jenny. "I wasn't going to let her . . . try and tell me what to do."[2]

Jenny's mother, Vicki Crompton, says her daughter never told her that Mark had gone from affectionate and charming to threatening and controlling. Instead, Jenny and her friends tried to handle it on their own.

She says she was shocked to hear teenagers at the trial say that slapping each other around was normal and that everybody does it. Not long after that, Crompton began visiting schools and talking to teenagers about dating violence.

"Sometimes the schools will say, 'We don't really think we have a problem, but we believe we need to educate [kids about it],'" says Crompton, author of *Saving Beauty from the Beast*. "Kids will come up later and tell me 'Yes, it is going on here. There is a problem.'"[3]

In fact, a survey conducted by Teenage Research Unlimited reports that a large number of teenagers between the ages of thirteen and eighteen not only are victims of dating abuse, but also accept it as normal. The problem gets worse as teens get older and involved in more serious relationships. There is tremendous pressure to have and keep serious relationships.

"The fact that significant numbers of teens are experiencing this behavior as normal is particularly distressing," says Paul R. Charron, chairman and chief executive officer of Liz Claiborne Inc., the company that helped develop the study. "Today's teens are our best hope to help create a society where intimate partner violence is simply not tolerated."[4]

Sexual Assault and Rape

What was supposed to be a fun-filled afternoon with friends turned into a nightmare for fifteen-year-old Holly. While her parents were out, she invited some friends over. These friends also brought along several other friends, including a young man about twenty years old.

When the young man disappeared in her home, Holly was concerned and went looking for him. When she found him upstairs, he raped her. But instead of telling someone, she kept silent. Like most rape victims, Holly felt guilty, ashamed, and confused.

"I had no words for what had happened to me," she says. "I just knew that I had never felt so lost or had such pain. My whole life had changed that afternoon."

Holly was an honor student. She was afraid that if anyone found out she had been raped, no one would be her friend. To cope with the trauma of rape, Holly kept herself busy with school and extracurricular activities. But after fourteen years of silence, Holly could not take it any longer. She knew she needed to talk about what had happened, so she found a counselor. Then she told her parents.

"It was so hard to admit I was raped, but once I said it, I finally learned to accept it. I finally said the word out loud," she says. "[My parents] couldn't believe I'd kept such a terrible secret. They wept for the child that was taken that day, and in the end telling my mom and dad brought us together."[5]

A Closer Look at the Problem

Physical threats and safety:

- Thirty percent of teens worry about their safety in a relationship.
- Twenty percent of teens in a serious relationship report that their partners have pushed, slapped, or hit them.

Controlling or abusive behavior:

- Sixty-four percent of teens have dated someone who was excessively jealous and asked where they were all the time.
- One in four teens in serious relationships said their partner kept them from spending time with family and friends.
- Sixty-one percent of teens said their partner made them feel bad or embarrassed.
- More than one in four teens have had a partner who called them names and put them down.

Sexual pressures:

- Twenty-nine percent of girls who have been in a relationship said they have been pressured to engage in sexual activity when they did not want to.
- Nearly one out of two girls worries that her partner will break up with her if she refuses to have sex.
- One in four teens between the ages of thirteen and eighteen says that sex is expected in their relationships.[6]

Every one hundred seven seconds in America, someone like Holly is being sexually assaulted. What's more, 44 percent of rape victims are under the age of eighteen. Yet despite these large numbers, sexual assault is severely underreported in this country. In fact, surveys indicate that nearly 70 percent of sexual assaults go unreported.[7]

Many teens think that rape only happens in dark alleys late at night. But being raped by a stranger is a lot less common than most might think. In fact, almost two thirds of all rapes are committed by someone the victim knows.[8]

For a number of young women, rape can be the horrific byproduct of dating. Some people think that date rape is about sex or passion. But rape has nothing to do with sex, love, or romance. Like other forms of abuse, it is about power and control, and it is against the law. Sometimes people think that a girl is asking for it because of her clothes or the way she acts. That is wrong, too. The person who is raped is not to blame. Rape is always the fault of the rapist.

The same is true when two people are dating. One person never owes the other person sex. Healthy relationships involve respect. When two people care about each other, they respect each other's wishes. They do not force or pressure each other to have sex. Too often when the victim knows the offender or has a relationship with him, a rape will be brushed off or downplayed with statements such as these: "Things got a little crazy," "We both had too much to drink," "We had already gone too far, so there was no going back," "She wanted it," or "It just happened." These phrases are excuses and often cause the person victimized to stay silent out of guilt and shame. But sexual assault should never be brushed off. It is a crime, and young people who have been raped need to find help and support.[9]

How Abuse Begins

Relationships usually do not start out abusive. Instead, they often appear very romantic in the beginning. The abuser often comes off as too good to be true and showers the other with lots of attention and acceptance. However, it does not take long for the control to begin. Soon, the attention becomes excessive and demanding.

Suggestions on what to wear and what not to wear might be followed by jealousy and accusations. An abusive boyfriend may

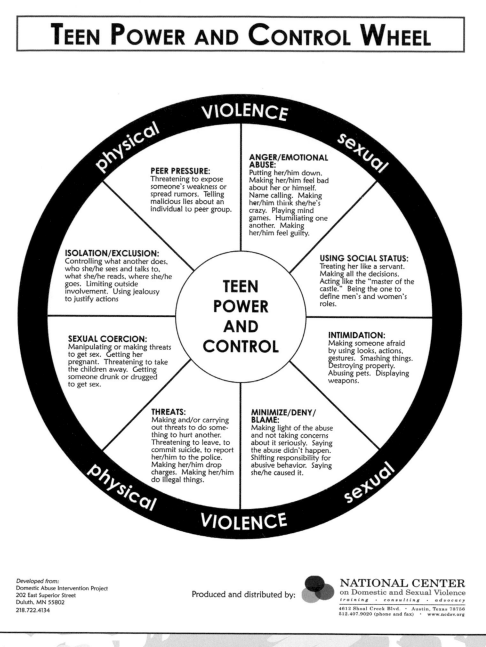

TEEN POWER AND CONTROL WHEEL

VIOLENCE

physical

sexual

PEER PRESSURE:
Threatening to expose someone's weakness or spread rumors. Telling malicious lies about an individual to peer group.

ANGER/EMOTIONAL ABUSE:
Putting her/him down. Making her/him feel bad about her or himself. Name calling. Making her/him think she/he's crazy. Playing mind games. Humiliating one another. Making her/him feel guilty.

ISOLATION/EXCLUSION:
Controlling what another does, who she/he sees and talks to, what she/he reads, where she/he goes. Limiting outside involvement. Using jealousy to justify actions

USING SOCIAL STATUS:
Treating her like a servant. Making all the decisions. Acting like the "master of the castle." Being the one to define men's and women's roles.

TEEN POWER AND CONTROL

SEXUAL COERCION:
Manipulating or making threats to get sex. Getting her pregnant. Threatening to take the children away. Getting someone drunk or drugged to get sex.

INTIMIDATION:
Making someone afraid by using looks, actions, gestures. Smashing things. Destroying property. Abusing pets. Displaying weapons.

THREATS:
Making and/or carrying out threats to do something to hurt another. Threatening to leave, to commit suicide, to report her/him to the police. Making her/him drop charges. Making her/him do illegal things.

MINIMIZE/DENY/ BLAME:
Making light of the abuse and not taking concerns about it seriously. Saying the abuse didn't happen. Shifting responsibility for abusive behavior. Saying she/he caused it.

physical

sexual

VIOLENCE

Developed from:
Domestic Abuse Intervention Project
202 East Superior Street
Duluth, MN 55802
218.722.4134

Produced and distributed by:

NATIONAL CENTER
on Domestic and Sexual Violence
training · consulting · advocacy
4612 Shoal Creek Blvd. · Austin, Texas 78756
512.407.9020 (phone and fax) · www.ncdsv.org

This resource is known as the Teen Power and Control Wheel. Each of the wheel's spokes contains a tactic used by abusers to control their partner.

try to control who his girlfriend hangs out with and demand that she spend all of her free time with him. As a result, girls may start to dress differently and stop hanging out with friends and family. They often believe that making these changes proves their love.

Put-downs, name-calling, and intimidation might surface, too. Eventually, the abuse may escalate into sexual pressures and physical violence. In fact, research suggests that after a teen dating relationship becomes sexual, there is a greater chance that verbal or physical abuse will become a factor. For instance, a recent study found that 74 percent of young people involved with an abusive partner said the abuse started after the relationship became sexual.[10]

Vicki Crompton believes that girls who do well in school and are respected by their peers are vulnerable to abuse because "they buy into the belief that they need a boyfriend." Abusers make an all-out attempt to destroy the young woman's self-esteem, she says. They want to be able to control her mentally and physically.[11]

In an effort to maintain the relationship, abusers will often use the good aspects to pull the victim back in after an incident. Most of the time, this proves successful because the victim is already attached to the abuser. Very few people would date someone who is abusive from the beginning.

Why Victims Do Not Tell

All types of abuse can be frightening. Yet many young people keep silent about it. In fact, two thirds of young people never report the abuse to a caring adult.[12] Feelings of shame and guilt often prevent teens from getting the help they need, says Robyn Lieber, education coordinator for the Council on Sexual Assault and Domestic Violence. In addition, the victim is often blamed for the abuse, she says.

For example, an abusive boyfriend might try to manipulate his girlfriend into believing that she caused the abuse. He might say things such as, "You made me hit you," or "If you had listened to me, this would not have happened," or "I told you not to wear that skirt again."

An abuser might also try to intimidate the victim with statements such as, "If you ever tell anyone about this, I will kill you" or "No one will ever believe you." These statements can make people feel too afraid to tell someone. Or they may feel like it would not do any good to tell someone about the abuse. Teens may also fear that they will lose some of their freedom if they reach out to a parent for help.

It is not surprising, then, that teens who have been abused by a boyfriend or girlfriend say they would discuss the matter with friends instead—much like Jenny Crompton did. Lieber says teens do not tell their parents out of fear that they will take over. "Their fear is that mom and dad are going to say, 'I told you so,'" she says.[13] Although teen dating violence is similar in many ways to domestic violence in adult relationships, there are some differences. For example, many teens have not had much experience dating. As a result, they may be susceptible to relationships that are not based on equality. For example, girls may try to be accommodating and allow

Boys Are Abused Too

When it comes to teen dating violence, the majority of victims are girls, but they are not the only victims. Studies reveal that one in five boys will experience some form of dating violence before they graduate from high school.

However, boys are less likely than girls to report being hit or called names. Some people speculate that boys remain silent because they are able to shrug it off. They do not consider a girl's abusive actions serious, hurtful, or intimidating. Researchers believe some of this has to do with the physical strength of boys in comparison to girls. Boys may believe that they could overpower the girl if things got out of control. Other times abuse may just be too embarrassing for a boy, so he stays quiet to avoid being labeled sensitive or wimpy.[14]

their boyfriends to make all the decisions in the relationship instead of offering their opinions or preferences.

Teens also tend to consider themselves in love in a shorter period of time than adults. Consequently, they have a harder time breaking up after just a month or so of dating. What's more, because abuse goes through a cycle, there are many times in the relationship when the abuser appears wonderful. So it can be hard for a teen to report someone they love. Sometimes when the abuser is apologetic or tries to make up with the victim with gifts, attention, or intimacy, both can mistakenly believe that their relationship is improved by their rough times. Feeling like they have been through thick and thin together makes them feel closer.

To complicate matters, when couples do break up, the victim often attends the same school as the abuser. This can give the abused teen the sense of being trapped and increase feelings of fear. Finally, the pressure to have a boyfriend or girlfriend can also play a role in whether or not an abused teen ends a relationship.[15]

Warning Signs of Abuse

Because many teens keep silent about abuse, it is important for friends and family members to be able to recognize the warning signs. Obvious signs of abuse are physical injuries. Poor attendance at school, failing grades, drug or alcohol abuse, and pregnancy can also be signs. Here are some other things to watch for:

- *Isolation.* Sometimes an abuser will attempt to isolate the victim from family and friends. He will control her time, including what activities she participates in.
- *Emotional Changes.* Once someone becomes abusive, the person being victimized will develop feelings of sadness and may appear desperate and incapable of making decisions. She may also cry more, have emotional outbursts, or want to be alone.
- *Constant Communication.* Many times, abusive people will call or text message the victim incessantly, and she feels she

must respond to him immediately. He might grill her with questions about where she is, what she is doing, who she is with, what time she will be back, and how many boys she has talked to.

- *Jealousy.* Abusers often struggle with jealousy issues and get extremely upset if the victim looks at or talks to another boy. He may even ask her not to wear makeup so she will not attract attention.
- *Background.* When a person comes from a home life that involves abuse, that could mean trouble in the relationship. He or she may have learned that problems are solved through control, manipulation, and violence.
- *Need to Impress.* Sometimes girls who have abusive boyfriends feel they need to take their advice about everything from friends and hairstyles to clothes and makeup. They may feel they need to prove their love, or they may be afraid of what will happen if they do not change.
- *Making Excuses.* People being victimized by abuse sometimes feel they must defend the abuser's cruel actions. An abuser may have convinced the victim that she is too sensitive, that she deserves what happens, or that she wants it.[16]

Bullying

Miranda thought they were her friends. She shared intimate details about her life with them, and she trusted them with her secrets. But it wasn't long until she realized that they were not friends at all. By the time Miranda was in eighth grade, the bullying started to reach an all-time high.

"I started to notice that they would put twists on my stories and try to make me look bad," Miranda says. "Then they started calling me names and pulling really mean pranks."

The bullying hit its peak when they created a pretend crazy hair day. The girls convinced Miranda to come to school wearing crazy hair and makeup with the promise that they would do the same.

Because teens do not have experience dating, they may be more likely to put up with abusive behavior. Anger and intimidation are never part of a loving relationship.

But when she came to school, she realized it had all been a setup. "I walked into the gym that morning, and the entire school laughed at me," she says. "Then they took lots of pictures."

From there the bullying progressed. The girls spread rumors and impersonated Miranda. For instance, they would write notes to other students pretending to be her. They were relentless with the name-calling and insinuations. Eventually, they were able to completely dismantle Miranda's reputation and leave her feeling hurt and hopeless. "Although I never really planned to commit suicide, I would have been okay with dying," she says. "I also started to self-harm and would cut myself."

The turning point for Miranda occurred when her mother and grandfather found out she had been self-harming. "All my life, I had never seen my grandpa cry," she says. "But when he found out I was cutting, he started crying. It was the first time I realized that people really cared about me."

Miranda's life turned around when she began attending vocational school and studying health care. Not only was it a fresh start for her, but she also did well academically in the new setting. And she loved the success. "I became addicted to that feeling of doing well and realized there were all these things that I could accomplish," she explains.

Miranda says it took a long time to overcome the bullying, but even though she still remembers what the girls did to her, she has moved on and is living a healthy life. She is no longer self-harming but is instead releasing tensions and stress by working out, eating right, and taking care of herself.[17]

At one time, bullying like Miranda experienced was the norm and was limited to the schoolyard. But today, bullying a schoolmate can be done via social media. Instead of a few notes passed at school, Miranda's impersonated messages could have been seen by the entire school on Facebook. Social media bullying poses big problems for millions of teens each year.

Cyberbullying

Today, the Internet plays a huge role in teenagers' lives. To many, life without it would be unbearable. They spend hours texting, tweeting, and posting to Instagram. They also use e-mail, instant messaging, social networking sites, blogs, and YouTube. But things can get out of hand when their talking turns into abusive attacks.

Increasingly, teens are using the Internet and other electronic messaging devices to threaten and harass their peers. One study found that 32 percent of all teenagers who use the Internet have been targets of some form of cyberbullying, including everything from annoying messages to threatening messages.[18]

Meanwhile, one in six teens say they have had private communication forwarded or publicly posted without their permission. Thirteen percent said that someone spread a rumor about them online, and 13 percent said someone sent them a threatening text or email. Six percent of teens have had an embarrassing photo posted online.[19]

"Sometimes kids think it is okay to be cruel online and that this is the social norm in some online communities," says Nancy Willard, director of Embrace Civility in the Digital Age. But, she says, kids need to be kind to other both online and off.[20]

Cyberbullying, which is sometimes called cyberabuse, can include:

- sending threatening e-mails or instant messages
- posting offensive comments about someone on a Web site
- sending harassing text messages via smartphones
- threatening or intimidating someone through electronic text
- pretending to be someone else while posting a message
- forwarding private pictures and videos to others.[21]

Teens need to remember that anything sent electronically to a friend can be forwarded to someone else or posted to a Web site without permission. A good gauge is to refrain from sending anything you would not show to your parents, your school's principal, or a church leader.

Predators on the Internet

Social networking sites, such as Twitter, Instagram, Facebook and YouTube, are popular among teens and college students. Individuals often use these sites to meet new people with similar interests. The sites allow them to discover more about themselves and connect with people who are like them. But networking sites, along with chat rooms, are also popular among online sexual predators. Teens can actually be interacting on these sites with adults who are pretending to be kids their age.

One of the biggest attractions of the Internet is that users can be anyone they want to be, but this is why it can be so dangerous. Young people do not always know with whom they are talking. They may *think* they know, but unless it is someone they know personally, they cannot be sure. Just because someone says he is a sixteen-year-old who likes to play the guitar and ski does not mean it is true even if he provides a picture. Predators often make up false identities and use pictures of other people to create fake profiles.

Teens run into trouble when they provide too much personal information in their profile or when they give personal information to someone they do not know. Predators often scan pictures looking for their type and will target kids who are having problems at home or in school. Once they find the person they are looking for, predators try to lure him or her into a conversation. They will comfort or sympathize with them to gain their trust. They may also buy them expensive gifts. Usually an online predator's ultimate goal is to meet in person, but they often want to do more than just talk.

As a result, teens should never meet privately with someone they have met online. To keep safe, teens should also use discretion when posting pictures on their profiles. And they should avoid discussing inappropriate topics or behaviors. Teens should also be careful about sharing their problems with people they do not know. Teens should control who has access to their accounts on Instagram, Twitter, and similar sites and only allow access to people they know in real life.

Many teens feel more comfortable communicating with strangers over the Internet. However, the person you think is an online friend may be a predator luring you into a dangerous situation.

Molestation: A Painful Secret

In 2012, Jerry Sandusky, a former Penn State assistant football coach, was convicted of sexually abusing young boys. All of the boys that Sandusky had initially befriended and then later repeatedly molested were from disadvantaged homes.

Prosecutors said that Sandusky used his charity, Second Mile, to scout for potential victims. Then he would give them gifts and money, invite them to his home, stay in hotels with them, and take them to Penn State games. Those who testified against him said that he assaulted them in hotel rooms, on Penn State's campus, and in the basement of his home. What's more, one of Sandusky's adopted children, Matt, came forward with stories of abuse, as well. But these crimes went unreported for years. The victims were men when they finally testified against Sandusky.[22]

Crimes such as these often go unreported because of the feelings that can develop between a child and his abuser. The molester or sexual offender works to establish trust and loyalty and gets the victim to like him or her. He or she may also threaten or convince the victim that they would both get in a lot of trouble if anyone found out. Guilt and shame also play a role in keeping a child from reporting the abuse.

According to Nicole Bromley, the average sex offender is a white, middle-class male in his mid-thirties who holds some sort of standing in the community. She adds:

> *I believe they use that standing in the community as a tool to gain trust and access to children. An example might include a Little League baseball coach who molests one of his players. A lot of parents in the community would never think that this favorite coach would do something like that. And for the child, it is confusing because they think, "Well, this must be normal because my parents really like this guy."*[23]

Bromley says a lot of people also believe the myth that sexual offenders are scary guys and you would be able to spot them right away. She says this is simply not true. Many sex offenders are respected members of their communities.

"The other myth that people believe is that sexual abuse only happens to poor city kids living in immoral families with bad parents and no friends," she says. "But sexual abuse is one act of violence that cuts across every single boundary there is: gender, race, culture, faith, socioeconomic status."[24]

Sexual Harassment

During the teen years, young people often have their first work experience. In addition to earning a paycheck, they learn about teamwork and responsibility. But sometimes teens learn a little more than they bargained for when they become victims of sexual harassment.

Such harassment can include exposing people to sexual jokes, as well as pressuring people to have sex and threatening them with job loss if they do not give in. Often those who complain are told they are just being too sensitive or that they do not have a sense of humor. Sexual harassment can be directed against men, as well as women. Like other types of sexual abuse, it is often about control, but it can be a matter of people not understanding what behavior is appropriate. Sometimes girls are harassed by older managers while others are targets of immature behavior by teenage and young adult supervisors.[25]

Many times, victims are reluctant to talk about what is going on. In one case, a young girl kept quiet for several months about the harassing treatment she received from coworkers and a supervisor. But her mom noticed changes in her daughter.

"She slept a lot, she was wearing baggy clothes, and she did not want to be touched," says Joan Ehrlich of the Equal Employment Opportunity Commission (EEOC) in San Francisco. "Finally her mother pulled it out of her," and the two filed a complaint. Eventually, the case was settled for $150,000 says Ehrlich.[26]

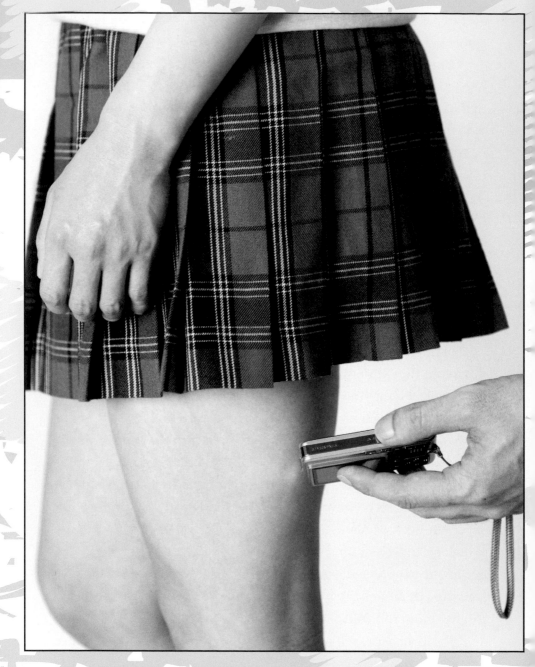

Sexual harassment is sometimes initiated by a teacher or supervisor. They use their power to make the other person feel uncomfortable and intimidated.

Sexual harassment can also happen at school. In fact, 80 percent of students will experience some form of sexual harassment while they are in school, according to the National Association of School Psychologists. While most are harassed by other kids, it is not uncommon for teachers and other school employees to sexually harass students at school. Kids who are sexually harassed can feel embarrassed, scared, and angry. They sometimes feel helpless to stop the harassment.[27]

Trafficking and Exploitation

Men and women who engage in trafficking of young people are skilled at spotting vulnerable girls at bus stops, in malls, or online. They can sense when a girl is feeling belittled, misunderstood, or deserted. Predators lure them with distorted love and false promises. Later they trap them with threats of violence.

"Any player can tell when a girl has the look of desperation that you know she needs attention or love," one Chicago pimp stated in a 2010 DePaul University study. "It's something you start to have a sixth sense about."

Rob Fontenot, an agent in charge of trafficking investigations with the North Dakota Bureau of Criminal Investigation, says that pimps are better at their jobs than some investigators. He also says they specifically look for wounded and hurting young victims. Contrary to popular belief, not all trafficking victims are from other countries.[28]

For instance, a three-year study funded in part by the US Department of Justice found that 75 percent of the children on the streets are white children from working-class and middle-class families. They also found that boys are victimized as often as girls. Even teens who become prostitutes willingly can be victims. Many times, these kids have been kicked out of their homes by their parents or guardians or have become too old for the foster care system. As a result, these "throwaway" kids find themselves on the streets with no home, no money, and no skills. They resort to prostitution just to survive and trade sex for food, shelter, and clothing on the streets.

Other groups of sexually exploited children include girls in gangs, children brought into the country illegally, and American youths trafficked nationally and internationally as part of organized sex crime rings. Many of those who solicit children for sex are married men with children of their own, the Department of Justice study reported.

"I think what the report highlights is that we're simply not doing a good enough job in this country taking care of our children," says Shay Bilchik of the Child Welfare League of America. "We've got to pay closer attention to the problem, including what's happening in our own homes and neighborhoods with kids who we think we're taking good care of."[29]

The High Cost of Abuse: How Teens Are Affected

Sixteen-year-old Amanda was excited about her date with Ryan. She really liked him. But she also was a little nervous about his party. She felt intimidated by his ex-girlfriend Claire. Not only was Claire a cheerleader, she also was popular, attractive, and likable. And she was going to be at the party.

This fact caused Amanda to worry about her relationship with Ryan. Was it possible that he really liked her, or did he still have a thing for Claire? After all, Claire was the one who dumped Ryan. So what would happen if she wanted him back?

To calm her nerves, Amanda had a beer. Then one beer turned into two beers, and two beers turned into four beers until Amanda had too much to drink. When her friends refused to let her have another drink, Ryan took her outside for some fresh air.

They had just started walking around the house when two football players from Ryan's school jumped out and attacked them.

One of the boys began hitting Ryan while the other dragged Amanda off. He pinned her against a parked car and began to rape her. She talked her way out of the situation, but as soon as he realized what she was doing, he knocked her across the top of the car and assaulted her again. Finally, she broke free and ran back to the house, but the door was locked. In a panic, she pounded on the door for someone to let her in. Just as the boy was getting near her, the door opened, and she fell into the house.

When her best friend asked what had happened, she lied and said, "He tried to rape me." But that is as far as it went. Amanda never told her friend she had been raped that night, nor did she tell her boyfriend, her parents, and certainly not the police.

After the rape, Amanda's life changed dramatically. She became promiscuous and started binge drinking and doing drugs. She also developed anorexia, an eating disorder, so she lost a lot of weight and showed signs of post-traumatic stress disorder. Post-traumatic stress disorder (PTSD) is an anxiety disorder that can develop when a person is exposed to a terrifying event in which physical harm occurred or was threatened. Traumatic events that may trigger PTSD include assaults, disasters, accidents, and military combat.

Amanda's symptoms of PTSD included becoming emotionally numb, losing interest in things she used to enjoy, struggling with irritability, and becoming more aggressive. Still, she never told anyone what had happened to her, and eventually her mind suppressed the memories.

Then something horrible happened. Amanda was raped again. At this point, her eating disorder changed. She began binge eating. "I was on a mission to make myself as unattractive as possible," she explains. "I also became very driven and refused to let anyone get close to me."

Finally, after twenty-three years of silence about what had happened to her, Amanda's memories began to surface. She had entered counseling for other issues and found herself dealing with suppressed memories of the two rapes. Today, Amanda is no longer silent. She talks openly about what happened and leads a recovery and support group to help other victims of rape.

"When a girl is raped, she needs to force herself to tell someone—her best friend, her mother, a close relative," Amanda says. "If girls do not talk about it, their lives will take a very different path. My life was shaped by two separate instances of what men did to me."

Amanda says it is the shame of what happened that keeps girls silent. "Shame is the first thing that attacks you—it's like a hook that sinks deep inside your soul, and it is the hardest thing to find healing for," she says. "Girls need to grieve over what they have lost. When you are raped, you lose part of yourself. You need help dealing with that loss."[1]

Impact of Abuse

Stories such as Amanda's demonstrate that the costs of abuse—no matter what the type—are often far-reaching and long term. In fact, studies have found that being abused can be more harmful during adolescence than at other times of life. Teenagers who have been abused often have more symptoms than those who are abused in childhood or adulthood.[2]

Beyond the cuts and bruises, teenagers can suffer serious consequences. Every form of abuse can impact their physical and mental health. It also affects their school performance and has been shown to lead to drug and alcohol abuse, teen pregnancy, and criminal activities. Abuse survivors may also struggle with depression and consider suicide. And they are more likely than those not abused to be runaways or homeless and to become involved in prostitution.

In general, abuse of all types traumatizes the victims. The resulting stress alone can hinder learning, damage emotional intelligence, and impact physical health.

Verbal and emotional abuse can leave even deeper scars than physical abuse. Abuse can affect development and have a long-term impact well into adulthood.

Physical Impact

Research has shown that abused children struggle with a number of physical problems, such as sleep disorders, hyperactivity, and attention disorders. They are also at an increased risk of suffering from PTSD.

Researchers are also finding that the fear and the stress young abuse victims experience can affect their developing brains. Evidence suggests that the brain's chemistry can be altered when an experience causes a harmful amount of cortisol in the brain. Cortisol is a hormone that helps the body respond to danger. Too much cortisol can cause memory lapses, anxiety, and the inability to control emotions. Abuse victims can also have high resting heart rates, temperatures, and blood pressure.

Moreover, some abused and neglected children regularly scan their surroundings for danger. They sometimes misinterpret the actions of others. "Children who are [afraid] can't take in cognitive information," says Bruce Perry, a child psychologist. "They're too busy watching the teacher for threatening gestures and not listening to what she's saying."[3] This type of behavior is due to the constant threats in the child's world. They are focused on the emotional and physical cues of other people, which is bound to affect learning.

Hidden Impact

Abuse experts often say that the impact of verbal and emotional abuse is often devastating to the victims. In fact, they argue that it can hardly be compared to physical blows because it often scars for life.

Author Patricia Evans, an expert on verbal abuse, says "standing up to a barrage of lies . . . is emotionally exhausting."[4] She says that teens who are verbally or emotionally abused often struggle to get a grip on reality because the abuser in their life is defining reality for them. As a result, they suffer from confusion, mental anguish, trauma, depression, an inability to focus, physical illness, or in some cases a complete loss of feelings. Evans says verbally and emotionally abused people almost always say, "No one can imagine what it is like, unless they experience it."[5]

Mental and Emotional Impact

Every person develops emotionally and psychologically. During that process, mental characteristics, such as intelligence, memory, recognition, attention, perception, and moral sense, are formed. Abuse impacts this process and can produce harmful effects. For example, if teens repeatedly experience something fearful or

CHILDREN COPING WITH FAMILY VIOLENCE

TRUANCY

NEW GENERATIONS OF VIOLENT FAMILIES

VIOLENCE AT SCHOOL

RUNAWAYS

TEEN PREGNANCY

Children Living in Violent Homes

VIOLENCE ON OUR STREETS

USE OF PORNOGRAPHY

SUBSTANCE ABUSE

SEXUAL HARASSMENT

FOOD ADDICTIONS

DATE RAPE

SEXUAL ASSAULTS

Developed from:
Domestic Abuse Intervention Project
202 East Superior Street
Duluth, MN 55802
218.722.4134

Produced and distributed by:

NATIONAL CENTER
on Domestic and Sexual Violence
training · consulting · advocacy
4612 Shoal Creek Blvd. · Austin, Texas 78756
512.407.9020 (phone and fax) · www.ncdsv.org

This graphic illustrates the impact of abuse on children. Children who live in violent households are at greater risk for teen pregnancy, substance abuse, and many other conditions.

unpleasant, their memory becomes fixated on that experience. As a result, they may recall or relive the misery over and over. Thinking about the abuse over and over can harm normal memory function.

Abuse also can cause lifelong problems, including low self-esteem, depression, and relationship issues. In fact, one study found that as many as 80 percent of young adults who had been abused as children had at least one psychiatric disorder by age twenty-one. These young adults also had a number of other problems. These included anxiety, eating disorders, and suicide attempts.[6] Additionally, they are four times more likely to contemplate suicide.[7]

Long-term abuse also can disconnect teens from their emotional selves. In other words, they learn how to stop feeling. And with the inability to feel comes a lack of empathy for anyone else. This is especially common among boys who survive abuse by shutting down their emotional awareness.

Loss of Identity. Young people who are abused also begin to embrace the messages they hear, such as "you're stupid," "you're fat," and "you're worthless." They begin to doubt themselves and feel inadequate and unacceptable. Consequently, they cannot see themselves accurately. They do not know what they feel or what they are really like.

When this happens, they may begin to look outside themselves for their identity. They may make up who they are based on what is cool, what will get respect, or what would look good. This appearance is created so no one will know what really happened to them.

Academic Issues. Teens who are victimized by abuse are less likely than nonabused teens to stay in school. If they do stay in school, they are less likely to get good grades.

"Educationally, I would say that 70 to 80 percent of the kids I worked with did not graduate from high school," says Beth Urban, a licensed social worker who works with abused teens. "They are much more at risk for dropping out . . . just because they get too involved in whatever's going on. Either the dating relationship . . .

is violent or at home there are too many issues. And parents a lot of times don't value education."[8]

Typically, abused teens have trouble concentrating and may develop learning difficulties. They may also have difficulty with teachers, which can lead to being expelled. Yet school could be one of the safest places for a teen. Teens who are expelled from school are three times more likely to be victimized than those who are able to remain in school. Research also shows that two out of three violent crimes such as rape or assault happen outside of school property.[9]

Impact on Behavior

When people think of behavior changes most commonly associated with abuse, they think of antisocial behavior and physical aggression. But abuse can also impact a young person's emotional stability. Abused teens are at risk for behavior problems, such as eating disorders, pregnancy, drug and alcohol abuse, and running away.

Eating disorders. Because abuse feels like a violation to the body—especially if the abuse is physical or sexual—many victims say they are not happy with their bodies. This unhappiness can then lead to eating problems. In fact, 32 percent of teens who have been physically or sexually abused have an eating disorder.[10] These eating problems can range from dieting episodes to serious eating disorders. The most common eating disorders include anorexia, bulimia, and binge eating disorder.

Anorexics have difficulty maintaining normal body weight; they have a fear of fat or weight gain and a distorted view of their bodies. Bulimics usually binge eat and then compensate with vomiting, laxatives, fasting, or excessive exercise. People who have binge eating disorder lose control of their eating and overeat at least two days a week.

There are a number of reasons why abused teens develop eating disorders. First, eating may be a way for victims to alter their bodies. They want to be less attractive or less vulnerable to abuse. They assume an altered shape will not be attractive to an abuser.[11]

Sometimes eating disorders are a way for victims to punish their bodies. By starving or by purging, they are "punishing the body that served as the abuse battleground," says Diann Ackard, a clinical psychologist whose practice focuses on people with eating disorders, body image disturbances, a history of abuse, depression, and anxiety.[12]

Eating disorders sometimes happen because the victim is trying to manage or control the impact of the abuse. "When feelings seem to be out of control, the abused individual may turn to their body as something to control," says Ackard. "Eating behaviors may be one of many ways that abused individuals attempt to regain some control over life."[13]

Teen pregnancy. Teens that experienced dating violence are six times more likely to become pregnant. They also are twice as likely to get an STD.[14] Sexually abused or assaulted females are also at risk for teen pregnancy. Research shows that girls with a history of sexual abuse were three times more likely to engage in prostitution and have children at an earlier age than girls who were not abused.[15]

Drug and alcohol abuse. Research shows that teens in abusive relationships may be more likely to develop emotional problems and substance abuse issues as they get older. For instance, girls who experienced dating violence as teens were more likely to binge drink and smoke. They also showed signs of depression and thought about suicide more than girls in healthier relationships. Meanwhile, boys who reported dating violence while teens were more likely to use marijuana. They also tended to be antisocial and think about suicide.[16]

Running away and prostitution. Many survivors of child abuse and neglect run away. In fact, 46 percent of homeless teens escaped a violent home and 17 percent left because of sexual abuse. These runaways are also more likely to participate in deviant behavior in order to support themselves on the street. By doing so, they increase their chances of being arrested and of becoming victims again. Many times, homeless teens are forced into prostitution. Or they

Research has shown that girls who are in abusive dating relationships are more likely to smoke and drink to excess. Eating disorders are also common among abused girls.

participate in survival sex, where they trade sex for food, clothing, drugs, money, or even a safe place to sleep.[17]

Escaping Unscathed

It is important to note that not all abuse victims suffer long-term consequences. In fact, outcomes can vary dramatically. Everyone reacts differently to trauma based on his or her personal strengths and weaknesses. Some people appear to escape unharmed, while others are deeply affected. This ability to cope and even thrive after having negative experiences is called resilience.

"Children, by nature, are resilient," says Beth Urban. "You will meet a lot of people in your life that when you hear their story [you think] 'Wow! You're kind of normal.' That's the resiliency."[18] There are a number of things that can cause a person to be more resilient than another. In addition to such personal qualities as self-esteem and optimism, protective factors include a strong community, access to health care, and having at least one caring adult in his or her life.[19]

Resiliency

Experts agree the risk that boys who grow up in violent homes will eventually become violent is great. In fact, 63 percent of boys ages eleven to twenty who are arrested for killing someone have killed their mother's abuser. Yet not all boys who witness domestic abuse will become abusers. Some are able to break the cycle of abuse. According to A Safe Place, a domestic violence crisis center, the factors that contribute to resiliency in boys include:

- How they interpret the violence
- How they cope with stress
- Whether supportive people are available to them
- Their ability to resist negative things in the home
- Being exposed to more positive things than negative things in the home
- Having strong self-esteem
- Having good relationships with peers

- Having a sense of hope
- Getting empathy and support from their mother
- Having hobbies, sports, or other creative activities
- Having a sense of control in their life.[20]

Some experts believe that one way to break the cycle of abuse is to help cultivate and provide the factors that lead to resiliency—especially in teens who are at risk for later becoming abusive.

All in all, much research has been done about the consequences of abuse and how to break the cycle. Sometimes the effects are mild; sometimes the effects are severe. Sometimes they last just a short time, and other times they can last a lifetime. But there is one thing that is absolutely certain—abuse changes the course of lives.

Abuse and the Community: A Look at the Impact on Society

In the Midwest, a young girl tells her mother that her father is molesting her, but he denies it. He claims she is just trying to get even with him. Then he punishes her for telling by tying her to a tree and threatening to kill her cat while she watches. To save her cat, the girl promises to be good and to take everything back.

In another city, a father ties his four-year-old son's hands behind his back because he was playing in paint. When the father, who is an alcoholic, passes out and forgets to untie him, the boy's hands are so severely damaged that they must be amputated.[1]

In Tampa Bay, a five-year-old girl dies after being thrown from a bridge by her father. He was already on probation from domestic violence charges.[2]

These stories are all true. Worse still, they are not uncommon. Yet the abuse of America's young people has been underreported and sometimes unrecognized for years. Although the rate of child abuse and neglect has decreased in recent years, nearly one in every one hundred children in the United States were abused in 2012.[3]

The reality is that many of our nation's youth are victims of abuse, neglect, and exploitation. Sometimes, they are even killed, abandoned, and sold. The kids most at risk are the ones from homes where the parents are poor or unemployed.[4] For instance, children in poor families have more than three times the rate of child abuse and seven times the rate of neglect than other children. Meanwhile, children whose parents are unemployed have about two times the rate of child abuse and two to three times the rate of neglect. Even living with a single parent and a live-in partner increases the risk of abuse. They are more than eight times as likely to experience abuse than other children.[5]

Some of the blame for the abuse of young people rests on society. Often people do not take teen abuse as seriously as they should. It is true that abuse is an ugly topic, and people do not want to think about it. But the more society tries to brush abuse under the rug and pretend it is not happening, the more validated abusers feel in behaving the way they do. If no one says to them that abuse is wrong and tells them to stop—and teaches them how to make good choices—they will continue to abuse. They may have no motivation to change because they often get what they want when they abuse another. Or they simply may not know how to change.[6]

Media serves as another powerful influence in how society sees violence and abuse. Television, movies, advertising, and music videos often sexualize teenagers and romanticize violence. As a result, violence against women and girls is sometimes considered normal.

Moreover, one study found that watching violence on TV can encourage kids to act more aggressively even fifteen years later. And the effect appeared in both sexes regardless of how aggressive they were as children. According to the authors of the study, media violence strips away a person's natural dislike for violence and sends a message that it is an effective way to deal with issues.[7]

Does Violence Breed More Violence?

People who study abuse often say, "Violence begets violence," which in many cases is true. For instance, when children are abused in some way, the likelihood that they will later be arrested increases. In fact, children who experience child abuse and neglect are about nine times more likely to participate in criminal activity. And about 14 percent of men and 36 percent of women in prison were abused as children. These figures are about twice that of the general population.[8]

Research also suggests that girls who are abused and neglected are at an increased risk of being arrested for violence as juveniles and adults. This was not always the case. But today, abused or neglected females are more likely than non-abused girls to be arrested for offenses such as drugs, alcohol, disorderly conduct, curfew violations, and loitering. What's more, nearly six in ten women in state prisons experienced physical or sexual abuse in the past. And 69 percent of those women said the assault occurred before they turned eighteen.[9]

Girls and Gangs

Tayshana Murphy was one of New York's best high school basketball players and a likely WNBA draft pick. But she had a secret. Murphy was involved in a street gang, and it eventually led to her death. She was gunned down in her Morningside Heights housing project by a rival gang.[10]

Experts say this case is an example of a growing national problem. Contrary to what most people believe, girls join gangs in large numbers. In the United States, experts believe girls comprise at least one quarter of all youth gang members. What's more, experts note that girls in gangs often use social media to spread insults and talk about who did what to whom.[11]

Some girls join gangs for protection, and others feel it is a sign of strength and equality. They have taken the message "If boys can do it, I can do it, too" to mean they can be aggressive, strike back, or be violent, too. This is especially true for girls who have been victimized or have grown up with violence.

System Failures

For years, the systems designed to address abuse often reacted to violence rather than attempting to prevent it. They failed to keep victims safe. Until recently, police lacked an understanding of the root causes and dynamics of abuse. The legal system did not provide them with what they needed to prevent and prosecute abuse cases.

Very few community resources were designed to help people dealing with abuse. Society considered abuse a private matter best left to those involved to work it out. While many of these problems have been overcome, there is still room for improvement.

For example, appropriate treatment and intervention programs need to be available. Unfortunately, teens with the greatest need often do not have access to high-quality treatment services with professionals who understand abuse. Those who have been severely traumatized by childhood abuse may need long-term counseling and care, but they may not have the money to pay for treatment.

Another problem with the system is automatically removing young people from their homes without considering other options. This strategy, while helpful in extreme abuse cases, is not always the best option and may not be safe. These young people can become victims again in their foster homes.[12] Some states solve this issue by requiring the offender to move out so the kids can stay in the home.

In addition, according to social worker Beth Urban, one of the toughest things for a teen is moving out of their neighborhood to live with a foster family in another community. Recently, child protective services has started recruiting foster families from neighborhoods where the kids are, she says.

"They can stay in their school, they can stay with their friends, they can stay inside [the community] where they have support," she explains. When kids are removed from their schools and their friends, "it's almost like they are being punished for talking about it [the abuse]."[13]

Unfortunately, most local agencies do not have enough money or a large enough staff to protect the young people who are brought to their attention. In fact, each week child protective services throughout the country receive more than fifty thousand reports of suspected child abuse or neglect.[14]

Not only is it costly to find a safe place for young people but also agencies often do not have the staff to address the problem. And there are a lot of expenses that have to be covered. These include costs to investigate abuse and to provide treatment, such as health care, counseling, and other services. There are also costs associated with law enforcement and the court system. All of this is taxing on the system. One report estimates that these costs are as much as $80 billion per year nationwide.[15]

Do Not Look the Other Way

Broken bones, bruises, and black eyes are usually what people think of when they hear the words "domestic abuse." But emotional, verbal, and sexual abuse can be much less noticeable and much more subtle. The effects can produce traits in victims that resemble those of hostages in life-threatening situations. The impact to the victim is not isolated. Its effects are far-reaching and impact the local community.

For example, abuse impacts local businesses and the economy. Abuse can make businesses less productive because of absenteeism, unemployment, and the increased use of the health care system. Some studies suggest that this costs the country $8.3 billion per year.[16]

Abuse can pose a threat to employees, and it can create security problems for companies. Keeping employees safe should always be a priority. Too often, victims mistakenly believe they must leave their job because of employers' fear for their safety. Employers are faced with recruitment and retraining costs when this happens.

Experts say that businesses should also examine their workplace policies. They need to review their security guidelines and determine if they are creating a safe environment. Employers should also watch for indications of abuse. Workplace supervisors might be the first to recognize the signs, especially if an employee gets harassing phone calls, an unwanted visitor, or is missing a lot of work. They can give the employee support and tell her about local resources. A statement as simple as "No one deserves to be hit" can provide vital support.

Everyone Can Make a Difference

Community members, such as educators, doctors, nurses, and clergy, can play a vital role in identifying and preventing abuse of both children and teens. The law says they have a moral and legal obligation to help by reporting abuse.

For example, nearly all children and teens are seen at some point in a health care setting. Whether it is for immunizations, sports physicals, or ear infections, young people usually go to the doctor. Therefore, it is important that doctors can recognize the signs of abuse and get the person the help he or she needs. They are also required by law to report abuse.

Even hairstylists, who are not legally required to report abuse, can have an impact. For example, a program called Cut It Out trains stylists and others in the industry to identify the warning signs of abuse. The program also equips them with the information they need to refer their clients to local resources, such as help lines, shelters, and support groups.[17]

Experts believe that when people such as doctors, teachers, and even stylists know what to look for and how to ask questions, they may be able to identify abuse at an early stage. The earlier abuse is identified and handled, the less impact it will have and the more

Physicians have a moral obligation to look for and recognize the signs of abuse in their patients. They are legally required to notify the proper authorities if they believe they have detected abuse.

likely healthy changes can be made. The same is true of other professionals who interact and work with young people.

Each year, though, teens who are victimized by abuse slip through the cracks in their communities. Only a fraction of them receive the kind of help they need. As a result, they are less likely to live up to their potential and contribute to their community. They are also more likely to wind up on drugs, pregnant, or in mental hospitals. The cost to society for failing these kids is enormous. The goal for every community should be that people are safe from harm. No community can flourish if its young people are not safe.

Ending the Violence:
How to Help and Get Help

When sixteen-year-old Carrie met nineteen-year-old Mark, she was drawn to him because he "was good looking and showered [her] with gifts." But that did not last. As it turned out, Mark was prone to anger, control, and abusiveness. "One day we were in the car . . . and the next thing I knew he . . . shoved the rearview mirror into my mouth and I was bleeding," she says.

Later, Mark apologized and even brought her chicken soup. But his brutality did not end there. He continued to frighten, humiliate, and beat her. Sometimes her bruises were so bad she would not change for gym class. Yet she stayed with him for three years. After she graduated, they moved in together and she got pregnant. And the violence got worse.

"It all finally came to a head when he . . . held [my daughter and me] hostage in the car for three days," she says. "We . . . drove around. No food, no stopping to go to the bathroom. We only stopped for gas and to feed the baby." When they returned home, Carrie was desperate for help. "I went . . . to call 911," she recalls. "He followed me and ripped the phone out by the cord and started beating me with it. Some people . . . called the police, and they put him in jail. It's taken me a long time," she says, "but I am starting to get my life back on track. I just want to be a good role model for my daughter."[1]

Teens such as Carrie are exposed to violence more than any other segment of the population.[2] Yet they are the least likely to report anything. They try to hide their scars—whether they are physical, emotional, or sexual. One study showed that only 38 percent of teen victims ages twelve to nineteen filed police reports while 50 to 58 percent of other people made reports.[3]

Helping Victims of Abuse

Most teens talk to each other about their problems. Therefore, it is important that friends know what to do when someone is being abused. Here are some recommendations:

- Do not ignore the signs of abuse. Talk to your friend about it.
- Express concern. Support your friend, but do not judge.
- Point out his or her strengths—many people who are being abused are no longer capable of seeing their abilities and gifts.
- Encourage him or her to confide in a trusted adult. Offer to go with him or her for professional help.
- Find out what state laws may protect your friend.
- Never get into a dangerous situation with the victim's partner or parent. Do not try to mediate or get involved directly.
- Call the police if you witness abuse.
- Do not try to handle this on your own. Tell an adult that you are trying to support a friend.
- Report suspected abuse to an adult you trust, such as a school principal, parent, or guidance counselor.

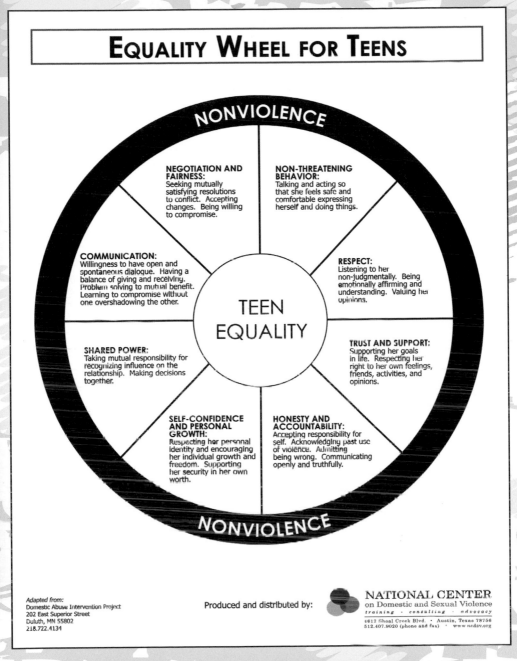

EQUALITY WHEEL FOR TEENS

NONVIOLENCE

NEGOTIATION AND FAIRNESS: Seeking mutually satisfying resolutions to conflict. Accepting changes. Being willing to compromise.

NON-THREATENING BEHAVIOR: Talking and acting so that she feels safe and comfortable expressing herself and doing things.

COMMUNICATION: Willingness to have open and spontaneous dialogue. Having a balance of giving and receiving. Problem solving to mutual benefit. Learning to compromise without one overshadowing the other.

RESPECT: Listening to her non-judgmentally. Being emotionally affirming and understanding. Valuing her opinions.

TEEN EQUALITY

SHARED POWER: Taking mutual responsibility for recognizing influence on the relationship. Making decisions together.

TRUST AND SUPPORT: Supporting her goals in life. Respecting her right to her own feelings, friends, activities, and opinions.

SELF-CONFIDENCE AND PERSONAL GROWTH: Respecting her personal identity and encouraging her individual growth and freedom. Supporting her security in her own worth.

HONESTY AND ACCOUNTABILITY: Accepting responsibility for self. Acknowledging past use of violence. Admitting being wrong. Communicating openly and truthfully.

NONVIOLENCE

Adapted from:
Domestic Abuse Intervention Project
202 East Superior Street
Duluth, MN 55802
218.722.4134

Produced and distributed by:

NATIONAL CENTER
on Domestic and Sexual Violence
training · consulting · advocacy
4612 Shoal Creek Blvd. · Austin, Texas 78756
512.407.9020 (phone and fax) · www.ncdsv.org

This graphic provides teens with the elements of a relationship based on equality. Compare it to the Power and Control Wheel on page 42 to see the difference in traits.

Helping Abusers

Typically, abusive people use excuses to justify their behavior. They will do everything they can to place blame on someone else. It is important to remember that abuse is not about anger, stress, drugs, or alcohol. To be a friend to an abuser, teens should focus on the fact that things such as hitting, name-calling, and demanding sex are wrong and hurtful. Hurting someone—whether physically, emotionally, or sexually—is never acceptable behavior.

When a teen has a friend who is abusing another person, here are some things that he or she can do:

- Learn about abuse.
- Talk to your friend about the behavior—but only about specifics that you have witnessed (such as the time he shoved his girlfriend at school or the time he called her names and made fun of her at a party).
- Do not talk about things the victim told you in confidence.
- Let your friend know that physically or sexually abusing someone is a crime and that making threats and stalking are crimes, too. (Does he really want a police record?)
- Tell your friend that abuse is wrong.
- Talk about places your friend can go to get help, such as a counselor, a coach, a pastor, or a hotline.
- Let him or her know that with help and a commitment to change, abuse can be unlearned.
- Report any abuse that you witness.
- Never try to mediate or get in the middle of an abusive situation.
- Tell an adult. It can be hard to be a friend in this situation, and adults can provide support and ideas.[4]

Getting Help

Teens who are being abused or who suspect that what they are experiencing qualifies as abuse need to be aware of their rights. Then, when they recognize that their rights are being violated, they

If a friend tells you he/she is abusing another person, listen to him/ her without judgement. Make sure your friend understands his/her behavior is wrong, and support him/her in finding help.

need to ask for help. One way for teens to be heard is to talk to an adult they trust.

"[Young people] should tell someone who will do the right thing—someone who will protect the [person being victimized] no matter the cost," Nicole Bromley says. "Sometimes the offender is someone in the community that other people might be afraid to report. So when you find the courage to tell someone, you don't want to be afraid that the person you tell will protect the offender, too."

Bromley also counsels victims to "tell and tell and tell" until someone believes them and helps them. "I also think that a child needs support in realizing the abuse is not his or her fault. They need to feel like someone is going to be there for them to talk to and that they are not alone," she adds.[5]

One option is to tell an adult who is required by law to tell the authorities. Strict child abuse reporting laws require certain professionals to report abuse. These professionals usually include teachers, principals, coaches, counselors, social workers, doctors, nurses, and members of the clergy. Typically, the law requires them to make an immediate telephone report. This call is then followed by a written report within a few days. As a result, teens can get the help they need.

Another option for teens is using a hotline when they do not have an adult to turn to. There are hotlines for child abuse, child pornography, trafficking, sexual exploitation, domestic violence, rape, sexual abuse, and incest.

Once the appropriate authorities have been notified, an investigation will take place and may result in the victim being moved to a safe location. To assist the victims, most states use a team of people in the investigation and treatment of child abuse cases. These teams combine the expertise of a number of professionals. For example, a team may consist of child abuse investigators, social workers, child psychiatrists, and legal professionals.

After the team understands the dynamics of the abusive situation and the type of abuse the child is experiencing, appropriate action is taken. In some situations, such as physical or sexual abuse, the parent may be arrested and eventually stand trial for abusing the young person. In other situations, a treatment plan may be developed. This plan could include requiring a parent to attend parenting classes or a batterer intervention program. Additionally, the team may change the child's living situation in order to protect the child.

States also are setting up child victim and offender registries. By doing this, officials will be able to see a pattern in complaints of child abuse or neglect. The goal is to make child abuse prevention programs more effective.

Navigating the System

In the court system, many states make sure the interests of a child are represented. For example, some states use court-appointed special advocates who are assigned to a child's case. Such an advocate, sometimes called a guardian ad litem, protects the best interests of the child. A guardian ad litem is a person appointed by the court to take legal action on behalf of a minor. The guardian ad litem also assists the court in making decisions about what is best for the child.

In addition, the Child Abuse Protection Act of 1990, passed by Congress, allows young people to submit victim impact statements. These statements tell the court how they have been affected by the abuse. Some states even allow children to submit hand-drawn pictures or letters to the court. Under this act, the term child refers to someone who is not yet eighteen years old. And each state is responsible for defining child abuse and neglect.

Finding an Escape

When the abuser is a dating partner, many times teens are confused and may not know how to deal with their partner's behavior. Threats and rage may be followed by vows of love. Abusers may also plead for forgiveness and promise to never do it again. Those who have been abused hope things will get better. Or they think that they can help their partner.

"A girl always has to be aware that if he can annihilate you emotionally and verbally, slice and dice you, you cannot be sure that he is never going to lay a hand on you," says Jill Murray, author of *But I Love Him.* Murray says girls also need to be cautious even if a boyfriend's physical violence is limited to walls, furniture, and other property. She says hitting walls is a classic sign that a teenage boy may become physically violent. "A boy who puts his fist through a wall or through a window is a dangerous person.. . . The next step [could be] he punches [her]," she says.[6]

Sometimes victims are afraid to tell someone about the abuse or to ask for help. As a result, many girls feel like they are stuck. But there are ways to get unstuck. These include making a break that is both final and definite and cutting off all contact. This means saying things such as, "I don't want a relationship with you," "I don't want to see you," and "Don't call me anymore."

Gavin de Becker, author of *The Gift of Fear*, says young people need to learn that "No" is a sentence. He believes the worst thing a young girl can do is "letting him down easy." In his book, he tells girls not to negotiate. He says after a decision to break up has been made, it only needs to be said one time. Any contact with the abuser after the rejection will be seen as negotiation, he says.[7]

However, ending a relationship with an abuser does not guarantee that the danger is gone. "The most vulnerable time for a girl [experiencing dating violence] is when she leaves," says Jill Murray. "[The girl has] taken their power and control back. And an abuser who does not have power and control is very frightened."[8]

Statistics show that 75 percent of all domestic violence homicides occurred when the victim was attempting to leave.[9] Escape from a violent partner is both complicated and dangerous and needs to be planned carefully.

Healthy Dating

As teens begin to date, they may find that it is fun and exciting to meet someone new. They may also discover that it is sad and difficult to break up. During that time, teens may also be learning what they like and do not like in a relationship. However, abuse and violence are never part of a healthy relationship. Teens can do a lot to avoid unhealthy or potentially abusive people by watching for particular behaviors. According to the National Center for Education in Maternal and Child Health, young people should be on guard if the other person:

- Wants to get serious quickly

Breaking off a relationship with an abuser requires decisiveness and firmness. Letting the abuser down easy may give him the impression that there is room for negotiation.

- Will not take no for an answer
- Is jealous and possessive or wants to pick his or her partner's friends and activities
- Is controlling and bossy—makes all the decisions, does not take other's opinions seriously, uses put-downs when alone or with friends
- Uses guilt trips (e.g., "If you loved me, you would . . .")
- Blames the victim for what is wrong (e.g., "It's because of you that I get so mad.")
- Apologizes for violent behavior (e.g., "I promise I'll never do it again.").[10]

Exploring Your Options

In most states, abused teenagers can apply to get a restraining order, which is sometimes called a protective order or order of protection. This order requires their boyfriend or girlfriend to stop abusing them. It may also state that the abuser cannot see or contact the victim. These orders are different in each state because they all define abuse differently.

Usually teens can apply for a restraining order even if they are under eighteen. Sometimes, though, the teen has to have an adult's name on the court papers, and the adult must ask for the restraining order on the teen's behalf. This adult does not always have to be the teen's parent. In some states, a judge can approve a restraining order if the person is another adult the teen trusts.

There are a few states that will allow teens to get restraining orders alone without involving the parents or another adult. These states typically require that the teen be at least sixteen. However, there are even a few states that let children as young as twelve go to court without an adult.[11]

Remember, restraining orders provide some protection, but they are not a guarantee. Some abusers may disobey the order even though doing so can lead to arrest. It is always a good idea for victims to plan as if the abuser will not obey it.

Planning could include changing class schedules at school, changing work schedules, and changing the locks at home. Other ideas include alerting appropriate people such as school counselors, teachers, and the principal, carrying a cell phone, staying away from deserted areas, and avoiding going places alone. Finally, teen victims should take all threats or stalking seriously and report them immediately.

Sometimes getting a restraining order comes after an arrest is made. Violence or the threat of violence is against the law, as are sexual assault, rape, and stalking. In fact, stalking is now a federal crime and has some stiff penalties.

If the police are called when a crime is committed or there is a threat of one, then many times the abuser will be arrested and spend some time in jail. It is likely, too, that a judge will issue a protective order and may require the abuser to attend a treatment program in addition to his sentence. These programs are often called batterer intervention programs.

More Ways Victims Are Protected

Many people who are sexually assaulted keep silent about their experience. In fact, an average of 68 percent of assaults are not reported.[12] As a result, states have taken steps to protect victims and encourage reporting. For example, rape shield laws keep the focus on the assault and the facts surrounding it. The goal is to take the focus off of the person victimized, including her past sexual conduct. For instance, rape shield laws keep attorneys from using the victim's reputation at trial. Usually, a hearing is held before trial to determine if any evidence concerning the victim's past is important to the case.

Also many states now have laws protecting the rape victim's comments to counselors. This was done so that those victimized do not have to fear having information about them revealed to others, especially the rapist and his attorney. Furthermore, most states no longer require proof that the victim attempted to resist the attacker.

And in all fifty states, it is now a crime to sexually assault one's spouse.

In addition to rape, stalking is another serious issue that is being addressed legally. Legal definitions of stalking vary from state to state. However, stalking generally includes actions that harass, frighten, and threaten the victim, such as following the victim, making threats, or leaving harassing messages. Sometimes the behavior even includes intrusions of time and space by the stalker— where the stalker shows up uninvited at the person's home, work, or a party. Some state's anti-stalking laws clearly prohibit both physical and electronic stalking. Others are not quite as clear.

Although the impact of stalking is sometimes downplayed by society, the actions of stalkers can be dangerous. Stalking can lead to violence, and those victimized often live in fear. Until anti-stalking laws were passed, victims had few options. Restraining orders were their only protection. As a result, many people were hurt and intimidated.

California became the first state to pass an anti-stalking law. Since then, all states and the District of Columbia have passed anti-stalking laws. These new laws give law enforcement agencies more powerful tools to arrest and prosecute stalkers.

The Interstate Stalking Act makes it a crime for anyone to travel across state lines to harass or injure another person. It is also a federal crime to use things such as the telephone or the Internet to encourage a child to engage in sexual activity. As for cyberstalking, the first US cyber-stalking law went into effect in 1999 in California. Some states include cyber-stalking in their harassment or stalking legislation.

Another piece of legislation designed to protect young people is the Victims of Trafficking and Violence Protection Act of 2000. New laws were passed under the act that allowed for bigger sentences for traffickers. It also provided resources for protecting and assisting those victimized and allowed many trafficking victims to remain in the United States and apply for permanent residency.

Many abusers who are angry at being broken up with stalk their ex-girlfriends or ex-boyfriends. Stalking includes following, leaving threatening messages, and frightening the victim.

Child protection laws will continue to grow and to change as states find better ways to keep young people safe.

Treatment for Abusers

In general, treatment programs are designed to reeducate abusers about their use of violence. Although the format and structure of the programs vary greatly, the programs typically educate the participants about what constitutes abuse and how to behave in ways that are no longer abusive. Two primary treatment programs include batterer intervention programs, which deal with physical, emotional, verbal, and sexual abuse, and sexual offender treatment programs, which are designed specifically for people who have sexually abused or assaulted another person.

Batterer intervention programs. Most programs offer weekly meetings where the participants discuss healthy and unhealthy relationships, sex-role stereotypes, and coping with anger and rejection. They also learn about power and control and what constitutes abuse.

Attending and completing such a program does not guarantee that people will no longer be abusive. The key to change lies in their ability to acknowledge their abusive behavior. Offenders must also be willing to accept that they alone are responsible for making a choice to be abusive. The victim did not make them do it. Nor is the problem a communication issue.

The goal of most programs is to keep the focus on the abusers and their actions. When a person chooses to hit someone, he or she is the only one who had control in the situation. With proper education, the abuser can learn to make nonabusive choices. Generally it has been found that such programs are more effective with teens than with adult abusers.

It is not uncommon for batterers to test the system. In other words, they may break group rules, miss required sessions, or be disruptive in group meetings. Experts recommend that when this happens, they be held accountable in immediate and meaningful ways. One example would be to remove a court-ordered attendee from the group, which could result in jail time. Another example might include requiring extra group homework or adding weeks to the attendee's length of participation. Not holding a batterer accountable may put a victim at risk for harm.[13]

In general, violent behavior is highly resistant to treatment. According to national research, court-ordered group counseling for adult men has little impact, and violence is often repeated. For instance, the improvement rate for abusive men is about 5 percent, according to Professor Christopher Eckhardt of Purdue University.

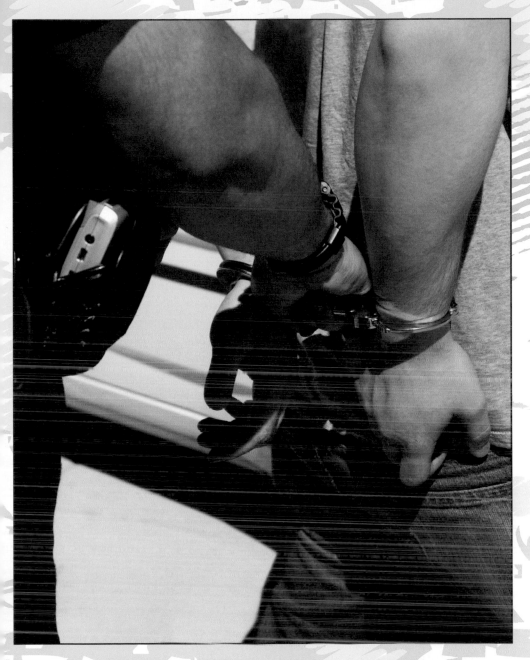

Help is available for teen abusers before their behavior escalates to the point of arrest and prison. Intervention programs that teach healthy behavior are sometimes effective for teen abusers.

"Five percent can translate into thousands of women who no longer have to suffer," says Eckhardt, "but it is not the magnitude we would like."[14]

Some experts believe that communities should develop similar programs for children before abuse becomes an ingrained way of resolving conflicts. They believe that violence prevention programs should begin as early as possible and progress through high school so abusive actions do not become acceptable.

Sexual offender treatment programs. Although sexual abuse and sexual assault is a major health problem, there is little known about what makes an intervention or prevention program successful. Nicole Bromley says that many times sexual offenders do not receive any type of treatment, even when they are in prison. According to Bromley:

> *It's different from state to state, but overall I feel this is an area where our justice system is really lacking. Oftentimes, sexual offenders do not receive treatment—at least not when it comes to an extensive intervention program. And I think offenders like incest sex offenders are able to stop their behavior if they are held accountable; if they are punished appropriately; and if they are given access to a high-quality therapeutic program.*

Yet because they do not receive adequate treatment and punishment, Bromley says that adult sexual offenders often become repeat offenders. And the rate at which they repeat their crimes is higher than any other area of criminal activity. "For example, 70 percent of adult sex offenders victimize between one and nine children, while 20 percent have ten to forty victims," she explains. "I don't think they have that many victims at once. Many times, they are getting in trouble and then doing it again."[15]

When it comes to adolescents who sexually offend, the numbers are somewhat different. For example, adolescents are less aggressive and less serious in their sexual offenses. What's more, young people who are guilty of a sexual offense generally respond to treatment. The rate at which they repeat their crimes is relatively low.

Moreover, many adolescent sexual offenders have themselves been victimized. Several studies have shown that adolescents who sexually offend are more likely to report being physically abused than to report being sexually abused.

Overall, some experts believe that the key to addressing sexual abuse and assault may lie in targeting young people more—with both preventative programs and intervention programs. In fact, experts such as Beth Urban feel that early violence prevention could break the cycle that leads to more violence in adulthood, such as domestic abuse and sexual assault.

"The one thing that I have always liked about teens was they are not as mentally formed yet as adults," says Urban. "As adults, we get much more set in our ways, set in our patterns, and it is a lot harder for us to change. . . . Sometimes there's a window between . . . middle school and high school . . . before you get the set-in-stone [behavior]. So a lot of times . . . they are ready and they are willing [and open to change]."[16]

No one would argue against the idea that young people have a right to be safe and healthy. But they do need help. Without help, they find themselves on a path toward a difficult future. Clearly it is important to identify and treat abuse, but it is also crucial to take steps so that future abuse can be prevented.

7

What's Next?
Addressing Abuse in the Future

Abuse leaves more than cuts and bruises on those victimized by it. Long after the bruises fade, the effects of abuse linger and tear at the soul. Logically, it makes sense that abuse victims are responsible for finding help, and abusers are responsible for changing their behavior. But what is the responsibility of everyone else?

Unfortunately, when faced with abuse many people do nothing. They are simply bystanders. They may hear or even see abuse happening, and still they do nothing. Neighbors, friends, and classmates tell themselves that they do not want to intrude or interfere.

But such inaction can mean years of pain and heartbreak for those who are unable to get out of a bad situation. They may not understand the abuse or know how to get free. In their powerlessness, they need others who are willing to take a stand and help them.

Abusers also need help. They may want to change but do not know how.

Lessons From the Past

For years, society did not see abuse as a significant problem. In fact, in the 1960s and 1970s it was considered progressive to treat family violence as a private matter rather than a criminal matter. For example, a 1967 police manual said that "in dealing with family disputes, the power of arrest should [only be] a last resort." Not long after that, the women's movement began working to change opinions about abuse, specifically domestic violence.[1]

As a result, the first shelters and hotlines for abused women opened in the 1970s. Additionally, several lawsuits were filed against police who did not protect victims of domestic violence. For example, in 1984 Tracey Thurman, a Connecticut woman, filed a lawsuit when the police failed to intervene while she was stabbed repeatedly by her husband. The US Supreme Court awarded her $2.3 million in damages. In many ways, this was a wake-up call for communities across the country. Some implemented mandatory arrest policies and prosecuted abusers even against the wishes of the victim.

Still, concerns about inadequate responses to abuse led advocates to push for federal legislation. In 1994, Congress passed the Violence Against Women Act, which was reauthorized and expanded in 2000. As a result, most states strengthened their domestic violence legislation.

Despite these improvements, advocates say there is still much work to be done. There is very little legislation to aid teen victims. Experts also cite improvements in education as a top concern. Connecting services and groups within a community and addressing the challenges within the legal system are other areas of improvement.

The Power of Education

Education is essential in addressing the issue of abuse and can serve three purposes. First, it is essential to make sure children and teens can identify abuse. Victims often feel isolated, powerless, disrespected, and misunderstood. Education is the first step in empowering young people to see that their worth is not tied to what another person says or does. Education also helps victims recognize that they have choices, and it gives them skills to handle their situation and helps them regain a sense of control in an out-of-control situation.

Second, education increases public awareness of the issue. It can also change public opinion. Some experts argue that abuse continues because communities have not made it unacceptable. People will say that abuse is wrong, but they look the other way. Creating public messages about abuse is an effective way to change this behavior. Then, this support can encourage politicians and other government officials to make changes.[2]

Third, education is needed to help those who abuse others, especially teens. Sometimes abusers can feel powerless to change because they have not learned any other way to behave. Through intervention programs and educational efforts, they can learn to make healthier choices when relating with others.

The most effective protection against abuse is to prevent it from happening in the first place. Many believe that education is the first step in doing that.

Connecting Communities

Abuse expert Beth Urban often says, "Young people grow up in communities, not programs."[3] What's more, when schools, families, and the community work together, there is a greater chance for success in addressing and preventing abuse. The more groups that are involved, the better the chance the information will click with young people.

Reaching out for help is essential if you are a victim of abuse. There are many places to seek help, including counselors, support groups, hotlines, and online communities.

One area of improvement is connecting abuse advocates, hospitals, police, prosecutors, and other groups that are often involved with abusive situations. Historically, these groups have not worked well together to help families who are experiencing violence. However, in recent years a number of communities are starting to improve their responses to families.

For example, the Center for Child and Family Advocacy in central Ohio was the first facility in the country where child abuse and domestic violence services were offered in one location. To accomplish this goal, the center developed partnerships with a number of local organizations, including Children's Hospital, local law enforcement and prosecutors, domestic violence organizations, children's services, and advocacy groups.

As a result, the center can offer many kinds of help for those victimized by abuse, including everything from preventive measures to long-term therapy and support. By doing so, they hope to not only provide top-notch intervention when it comes to abuse but also to become a leader in preventing abuse. This type of cutting-edge intervention is now being used in four hundred communities nationwide.

"Putting the child at the center is important," says Urban. "Typically, when child abuse happens the police are called, social workers are called, and the kid has to go to the hospital. It is like re-victimizing the child in several different steps." When the services are centralized, she says, everybody comes to the child, and it is much easier on him or her because the child only has to go one place.

Urban says the center is based on a national model known as the Family to Family model. This model has four basic beliefs: (1) a child's safety is the top concern; (2) children belong in families; (3) families need strong communities; and (4) child welfare systems need to partner with the community and with others. The ultimate goal of the Family to Family model is to preserve the family while understanding the needs of the child.[4]

Make a Difference

Another way to combat abuse is for ordinary people to get more involved. This can be done by volunteering to work at shelters, answering hotline phones, or by participating in mentoring groups like Big Brother Big Sister.

The CASA program is another option. CASA, which stands for Court Appointed Special Advocates, is an organization of volunteers who become appointed members of the court. They help keep abused and neglected children from slipping through the cracks.

Today, there are 951 state and local program offices nationwide. CASA programs across the country are known by several different names, including Guardian ad Litem, Child Advocates, and Voices for Children.[5] Once assigned, the guardian's job is to do research, says Holli Litwiller, a guardian ad litem in the program. This is done by meeting with the children and by going through any written material, such as criminal records and family care plans.

"Typically, I meet with the children at least once a month from the beginning of the case until it is closed," says Litwiller. She notes that the guardian also speaks with anyone who has regular contact with the child and attends court on behalf of the child when there is a hearing. The purpose is to relay the child's wishes to the judge. Guardians also share what they think would be best for the children.

"It helps children to give them a voice in court," says Litwiller. "The guardian ad litem is different from the case worker in that they don't really take into consideration what the parents want. They . . . just focus on what the child wants and what's in their best interest. Volunteers normally have more compassion and are passionate about serving the child and making sure the best decision is made for him or her."

Litwiller adds that children who get assigned a CASA volunteer are less likely to enter the foster care system. "They are less likely to . . . be included in all the negative statistics that come with homes that have neglect and abuse," she says. "So they do better educationally, socially, emotionally."[6]

Faith-Based Help

Two out of every three Americans are affiliated with a faith-based group, and one out of four Americans is an active member of such a group. As a result, it is not surprising that many young people go to religious leaders for help.[7]

Some churches, temples, mosques, and synagogues handle abusive situations well. They provide both practical and spiritual guidance and sometimes make referrals to other organizations. However, there are still those who are ill equipped to deal with abuse.

"[In the past], churches have been unprepared to truly understand the difference between a batterer and an angry person or the issue of addressing emotional and verbal abuse on a consistent basis," says Ron Hitchcock, a marriage and family life pastor at Vineyard Church of Columbus, Ohio. "But we believe the faith-based community is beginning to do well in response to domestic violence. We're working with community organizations to address the issue. We're not as suspect of each other as in the past."

Hitchcock, whose church has a weekly attendance of more than seven thousand people, says many times a church can offer victims and abusers resources that community groups cannot. Conversely, community groups can offer resources that churches cannot. "The church's strength is reconciliation," he says. "In fact, the gospel declares that the ministry of reconciliation has been given to the church for the world." If churches can show others what reconciliation looks like, he believes that together they can provide a more holistic approach to recovery.

"Domestic violence is not about class, it's not about money, it's about human brokenness," he says. "It's about a brokenness of humanity that reflects their need for [God]. And this is not a new thing; it's been with humanity since day one."

Hitchcock says his church is in the process of implementing groups for abusers and victims. One distinction his church will make is to separate the batterers from those who are emotionally abusive.

Consider turning to your place of worship for guidance. Their leaders and member networks can be valuable resources for victims of abuse, both practically and spiritually.

He says the church has found that when emotionally abusive men are placed with physically violent men, those who emotionally abuse others are more resistant to change. "[When they are together] you lose the ability to help them to see where the emotional and verbal abuse are contrary to the Scriptures because they say 'I'm not a batterer!' [and they resist help]," he says.

Hitchcock says that by developing training for members and building a program to address the issue, faith-based communities can strengthen their role in ending abuse.[8]

Seeking Justice

Dealing with abuse in court is a daunting task. Court calendars are full. Probation officers are overworked. Social workers are stretched too thin. Judges do not always have access to vital information. These factors all make handling abuse cases a challenge. Yet despite these challenges, those in the legal system have a responsibility to keep those victimized by abuse safe while ensuring their abusers are held accountable.

Abuse cannot be ignored. It is a huge national problem that is not going to go away. To address these issues, many state courts and other organizations are developing task forces to try to improve the legal system's response to abuse. California has one such task force led by Judge Laurence D. Kay. The goal is to provide a way for the community to give the courts feedback.

Additionally, Judge Kay says that courts, such as those in California, need systems in place to give them information, resources, and staff. These things, he says, will aid in providing the victim safety and the abuser accountability. "This means that computers must talk to each other," he says. "It means that judges must have access to information. And it means that judges must be able to respond effectively to the differing needs of each individual case."[9]

Judge Kay says the key elements of such a program include:
1. Resources for education and technology

2. Communication within the court and feedback from the public
3. Leadership from judges and others in the court
4. Accountability, monitoring, and ongoing assessments of court performance.

Abuse affects all of us, and it is not uncommon, says Judge Kay. "Although we may not see it, it is all around us—in our families, in our neighborhoods, in our schools, in our places of work. . . ." he says. "[When] we fail to do everything possible to treat [abuse] cases as a continuing and serious public safety risk . . . we are letting down these victims as well as our society."[10]

There are no quick fixes when it comes to abuse. But by being aware of abuse and taking a stand when appropriate, you can do a lot to prevent abuse in your community.

Chapter Notes

Chapter 1. The Quest for Power and Control: Understanding Abuse

1. Interview with [name withheld], December 2014.

2. Interview with Nicole Braddock Bromley, January 2008.

3. Patricia Evans, *Teen Torment* (Avon, Mass.: Adams Media Corporation, 2003), pp. 7, 57.

4. Kali Munro, "Emotional Abuse: The Most Common Form of Abuse," Kalimunro.com., 2001, <http://www.kalimunro.com/article_emotional_abuse.html> (January 17, 2008).

5. Cindy C., "Emotional Abuse—What is it?" Helping Teens, October 14, 2003, <www.helpingteens.org/common/print.php> (September 30, 2006).

6. Interview with Nicole Braddock Bromley, January 2008.

Chapter 2. Houses of Pain: Abuse Inside the Home

1. Interview with [name withheld], May 2007.

2. Melissa McEver, "Self-Abuse More Likely Among Teens with Low Self-Esteem, Anxiety," *The Brownsville Herald*, June 12, 2005, <www.brownsvilleherald.com/ts_more.php?id=65663_0_10_0_C> (September 29, 2006).

3. "Spanking Research," Dr. Phil, n.d., <http://www.drphil.com/articles/print/?ArticleID=256> (February 25, 2008).

4. "Should spanking your child be illegal?" *ABC News*, November 28, 2007, <http://abcnews.go.com/GMA/story?id=3924024> (January 28, 2008).

5. "Self-Injury in Adolescents," American Academy of Child and

Adolescent Psychiatry, <http://www.aacap.org/AACAP/Families_ and_Youth/Facts_for_Families/Facts_for_Families_Pages/Self_ Injury_In_Adolescents_73.aspx> (January 2015).

6. Interview with Nicole Braddock Bromley, January 2008.

7. "Child Molestation at a Glance," Child Molestation Laws, n.d., <www.childmolestationlaws.com> (October 16, 2006).

8. "Incest," The National Center for Victims of Crime, n.d., <www. ncvc.org/ncvc/main.aspx?dbName=DocumentViewer&Document ID=32360> (October 16, 2006).

9. Ibid.

10. Interview with Nicole Braddock Bromley, January 2008.

11. Ibid.

12. "Child Sexual Abuse," National Center for Victims of Crime, 2004, <www.ncvc.org> (September 30, 2006).

13. Interview with [name withheld], January 2008.

14. "Domestic Violence Facts," National Coalition Against Domestic Violence, n.d., <www.ncadv.org/files/domesticviolencefacts.pdf> (March 13, 2008).

15. "Information on Domestic Violence," Domestic Abuse Shelter of the Florida Keys, n.d., <www.domesticabuseshelter.org/Info DomesticViolence.htm> (April 1, 2008).

16. "Intimate Partner Violence in the United States," Bureau of Justice Stasics, US Department of Justice, December 19, 2007, <http:// www.ojp.usdoj.gov/bjs/intimate/ipv.htm> (April 14, 2008).

17. "Domestic Violence Facts."

18. "Identifying and Responding to Domestic Violence: Consensus Recommendations for Child and Adolescent Health," pp. 11–12, Family Violence Prevention Fund, August 2004, <http://endabuse. org/programs/healthcare/files/Pediatric.pdf> (January 28, 2008).

19. "The Facts on Children and Domestic Violence," Futures Without

Violence, <http://www.futureswithoutviolence.org/userfiles/file/ Children_and_Families/Children.pdf> (January 2015).

20. "Effects on Children Who Live With Domestic Violence," A Safe Place, n.d., <http://www.asafeplaceforhelp.org/childreneffects. html> (September 29, 2006).

21. "Domestic Violence and Homelessness," National Coalition for the Homeless, <http://www.nationalhomeless.org/factsheets/ domestic.html> (January 2015).

22. "The Impact of Family Violence on Children," Focus on the Family, 2004, <www.family.org/fmedia/misc/a0034023.cfm> (October 17, 2006).

Chapter 3. Unhealthy Relationships: Abuse Outside the Home

1. Vicki Crompton and Ellen Zelda Kessner, *Saving Beauty from the Beast: How to Protect Your Daughter from an Unhealthy Relationship* (Boston, Mass.: Little, Brown and Company, 2003), pp. 3–5.

2. "A Mother's Story," *CBS News*, July 30, 2003, <www.cbsnews.com/ stories/2003/07/29/60II/printable565639.shtml> (March 16, 2007).

3. Ibid.

4. "EDC's Teen Dating Violence Curriculum Hailed by U.S. Senators," Education Development Center, April 2006, <http://main.edc.org/ Newsroom/features/abuse.asp> (March 16, 2007).

5. Ibid

6. "Survivor Stories," The Voices and Faces Project, n.d., <www.voices andfaces.org/survivor_holly.asp> (June 27, 2007).

7. "Statistics and Key Facts," Rape, Abuse and Incest National Network, <http://www.rainn.org/statistics/> (January 2015).

8. Ibid.

9. "Survivor Stories."

10. Heidi Splete, "Sex Often Precedes Violence," *Clinical Psychiatry News*, June 2005, p. 33.

11. Joanne Richard, "Obsessive Love: A Mother's Harrowing Account of the Death of her Daughter and the Power of Forgiveness," *The Sun*, February 27, 2005, <http://lifewise.canoe.ca/SexRomance/2005/02/27/pf-944512.html> (March 16, 2007).

12. Pat Burson, "Love Sick: When Teen Relationships Become Abusive, Sometimes No One Else Knows," *Newsday*, June 13, 2005, <www.ncdsv.org/images/LoveSickWhenTeenRelationships.pdf> (January 28, 2008).

13. Dolly A. Butz, "Violence in Relationships Fact of Life for Many Teens," *Sioux City Journal*, October 2, 2005, <www.siouxcity journal.com/articles/2005/10/02/news/local/3ff2112a820bd4ae8625708 e000ee7cc.txt> (March 16, 2007).

14. "Learning About Dating Violence: Why It Matters," Break the Cycle, <http://www.breakthecycle.org/why-it-matters> (January 2015).

15. Shannon Barry, "General Information on Teen Dating Violence," <http://www.abuseintervention.org/TeenDatingViolence.doc> (February 25, 2008).

16. Jill Murray, "Warning Signs of Teen Dating Abuse," *The Oprah Winfrey Show*, 2008, <www.oprah.com/tows/pastshows/tows_2002/tows_past_20020228_b.jhtml> (February 25, 2008).

17. Interview with Miranda Vandagriff (January 2015)

18. Joan E. Lisante, "Cyber Bullying: No Muscles Needed," Connect For Kids, June 6, 2005, <www.connectforkids.org/node/3116/ print> (May 7, 2007).

19. "Cyberbullying," PewResearch Internet Project, <http://www.pewinternet.org/2007/06/27/cyberbullying/> (January 2015).

20. Ibid.

21. "Beware of the Cyber Bully," i-SAFE America Inc., n.d., <www. isafe. org/imgs/pdf/education/CyberBullying.pdf> (January 29, 2008).

22. Drape, Joe. "Sandusky Guilty of Sexual Abuse of 10 Young Boys," *The New York Times*, June 22, 2012. <http://www.nytimes. com/2012/06/23/sports/ncaafootball/jerry-sandusky-convicted-of-sexually-abusing-boys.html?_r=1& > (January 2015).

23. Interview with Nicole Braddock Bromley, January 2008.

24. Ibid.

25. Stacy A. Teicher, "Workplace Harassment of Teens," *CBS News*, March 3, 2005 (originally published in the *Christian Science Monitor*), <www.cbsnews.com/stories/2005/03/03/national/printable677789.shtml> (September 30, 2006).

26. Ibid.

27. "Sexual Harassment," National Association of School Psychologists, <http://www.nasponline.org/educators/Sexual%20Harassment. pdf> (January 2015).

28. Lymn, Katherine, "North Dakota Sex Trafficking: Pimps Rule the Game," TwinCities.com/Pioneer Press, January 5, 2015, <http:// www.twincities.com/nation/ci_27260275/n-dakota-sex-trafficking-pimps-rule-game> (January 2015).

29. "Study: Child Sex Abuse 'Epidemic' In U.S.," CNN.com Law Center, September 11, 2001, <http://archives.cnn.com/2001/ LAW/09/10/child.exploitation/> (June 27, 2007).

Chapter 4. The High Cost of Abuse: How Teens Are Affected

1. Interview with [name withheld], May 2007.

2. Madeline Wordes and Michell Nunez, "Our Vulnerable Teenagers: Their Victimization, Its Consequences, and Directions for Prevention and Intervention," p. ii, The National Center for Victims of Crime and the National Council on Crime and Delinquency,

May 2002, <http://www.ncvc.org/ncvc/AGP.Net/Components/ documentViewer/Download.aspxnz?DocumentID=3>2558 (March 31, 2008).

3. Shannon Brownlee, "The Biology of Soul Murder: Fear Can Harm a Child's Brain; Is It Reversible?" *U.S. News & World Report*, vol. 121, no. 19, November 11, 1996, p. 71.

4. Patricia Evans, *Teen Torment* (Avon, Mass.: Adams Media Corporation, March 2003), p. 65.

5. Brownlee.

6. Ibid., p. 68.

7. "Long-Term Consequences of Child Abuse and Neglect," Child Welfare Information Gateway, April 2006, <www.childwelfare. gov/ pubs/factsheets/long_term_consequences.cfm> (January 25, 2008).

8. "Identifying and Responding to Domestic Violence: Consensus Recommendations for Child and Adolescent Health," Family Violence Prevention Fund, August 2004, <http://endabuse.org/ programs/healthcare/files/Pediatric.pdf> (January 28, 2008).

9. Interview with Beth Urban, licensed social worker, May 2007.

10. Wordes and Nunez, p. i.

11. "Identifying and Responding to Domestic Violence: Consensus Recommendations for Child and Adolescent Health."

12. Ibid.

13. Diann M. Ackard, "Physical and Sexual Abuse of Teens Linked to Eating Disorders," *Paradigm*, Spring 2002, p. 9, <http://www. onlineparadigm.com/archive/parent_interest/mental_health/ eating_disorders/Eating%20Disorders%20and%20Abuse.pdf> (February 25, 2008).

14. Ibid.

15. Wordes and Nunez, p. 13.

16. Ibid.

17. "Homeless Youth & Teen Statistics", Safe Horizon, www.safehorizon. org/page//streetwork-homeless-youth-facts-69.html (May 2015)

18. Interview with Beth Urban, licensed social worker, May 2007.

19. "Long-Term Consequences of Child Abuse and Neglect," p. 3.

20. "Children and Domestic Violence."

Chapter 5. Abuse and the Community:
A Look at the Impact on Society

1. Karen Polonko, "Child Abuse and Neglect—The need for courage," *Quest,* Fall 2005, pp. 26–27, <http://www.odu.edu/ao/ instadv/ quest/childabuse.pdf> (January 29, 2008).

2. "Father Facing Murder Charges After 5-Year-Old Girl Thrown from Tampa Bridge," *Fox News,* January 8, 2015, < http://www.foxnews. com/us/2015/01/08/5-year-old-dies-after-being-thrown-from bridge-florida-police say/> (January 2015).

3. National Child Abuse and Neglect Data System. Child Maltreatment 2012, <http://www.acf.hhs.gov/programs/cb/resource/child-maltreatment-2012> (January 2015).

4. US Dept of Health and Human Services. Fourth National Incidence Study of Child Abuse and Neglect. Report to Congress. <http:// www.acf.hhs.gov/programs/opre/abuse_neglect/natl_incid/index. html> (January 2015).

5. Ibid.

6. Rachel Baldino, "Emotional Abuse in Teen Dating Relationships: What Every Parent Needs to Know," SixWise, n.d., <www.sixwise. com/display/PrintPage.aspx?DocID=725&&PrintPage=yes> (October 15, 2006).

7. Vries, Lloyd. "Study: TV Violence Begets Violence," *CBS News*, < http://www.cbsnews.com/news/study-tv-violence-begets-violence/> (January 2015).

8. "Child Abuse Statistics and Facts," ChildHelp, <https://www.childhelp.org/child-abuse-statistics/> (January 2015).

9. Sipes Jr., Leonard A. "Statistics on Women Offenders," Corrections.com, February 4, 2013, <http://www.corrections.com/news/article/32408-statistics-on-women-offenders> (January 2015).

10. Hamilton, Brad. "Rise of the Girl Gangs," *New York Post*, December 4, 2011, <http://nypost.com/2011/12/04/rise-of-the-girl-gangs/> (January 2015).

11. Ibid.

12. "Violence and the Family: Report of the APA Presidential Task Force on Violence and the Family," American Psychological Association, 2006, <www.apa.org/pi/viol&fam.html> (October 17, 2006).

13. Interview with Beth Urban, licensed social worker, May 2007.

14. "Child Abuse Prevention: An Overview," p. 5, US Department of Health and Human Services, 2002, <www.preventchildabuse.org/publications/cap/cap_2003/2003_1.pdf> (January 29, 2008).

15. "Estimated Annual Cost of Child Abuse and Neglect," Prevent Child Abuse America, April 2012, <https://www.preventchildabusenc.org/assets/preventchildabusenc/files/cms/100/1299.pdf> (January 2015).

16. Pearl MD, Robert. "Domestic Violence: The Secret Killer that Costs $8.3 Billion Annually," *Forbes*, December 5, 2013, <http://www.forbes.com/sites/robertpearl/2013/12/05/domestic-violence-the-secret-killer-that-costs-8-3-billion-annually/> (January 2015).

17. "Cut It Out: Salons Against Domestic Abuse," n.d., <www.cutitout.org> (January 25, 2008).

Chapter 6. Ending the Violence: How to Help and Get Help

1. Vanessa Bush, "A Thin Line Between Love and Hate," *ESSENCE*, November 2002, pp. 195–196.

2. "Teens Are Exposed to Violence More Than Any Other Segment of Our Population," National Child Assault Prevention Project, n.d., <http://www.ncap.org/programs/descriptions/teen.html> (June 27, 2007).

3. "Reaching and Serving Teen Victims: A Practical Handbook," National Crime Prevention Council, 2005, <http://www.ncpc. org/cms/cms-upload/ncpc/files/Teen%20Victims.pdf> (January 29, 2008).

4. "Teen Dating Abuse," Office For Women, n.d., <www.westch estergov.com/women/datingabuse1.htm> (October 15, 2006).

5. Interview with Nicole Braddock Bromley, January 2008.

6. "Tragic Tale of Teen Dating Violence," *ABC News*, November 10, 2006, <http://abcnews.go.com/2020/print?id=630874> (March 16, 2007).

7. Vicki Crompton and Ellen Zelda Kessner, *Saving Beauty From the Beast: How to Protect Your Daughter From an Unhealthy Relationship* (Boston, Mass.: Little, Brown and Company, 2003) pp. 52–53.

8. "Tragic Tale of Teen Dating Violence."

9. Domestic Abuse Shelter of the Florida Keys, <http://www. domesticabuseshelter.org/InfoDomesticViolence.htm> (January 2015).

10. Crompton.

11. "Legal Information on Teen Dating Violence," Women's Law, n.d., <www.womenslaw.org/teens.htm#16> (May 7, 2007).

12. "Reporting Rates," Rape, Abuse and Incest National Network, <https://www.rainn.org/get-information/statistics/reporting-rates> (January 2015).

13. Mary Jane Happy, "Domestic Violence Hurts Kids," *Press & Guide*, July 17, 2005, <http://pressandguide.com/stories/071705/loc_20050717003.shtml> (October 15, 2006).

14. Mark Ellis, "Futile Effort, or Worth a Try?: Group counseling seldom effective in stemming domestic violence," *Columbus Dispatch*, September 17, 2006.

15. Interview with Nicole Braddock Bromley, January 2008.

16. Interview with Beth Urban, licensed social worker, May 2007

Chapter 7. **What's Next? Addressing Abuse in the Future**

1. Cathy Young, "Domestic Violence: An In-Depth Analysis, Independent Women's Forum, September 30, 2005, <http://www.iwf.org/news/show/19011.html> (February 25, 2008).

2. "Prevention Strategies," Stop Violence Against Women, May 2007, <http://www1.umn.edu/humanrts/svaw/domestic/explore/9prevention.htm> (May 13, 2007).

3. Interview with Beth Urban, licensed social worker, May 2007.

4. Ibid.

5. "History of the CASA Movement," Court Appointed Special Advocates (CASA), n.d., <www.nationalcasa.org/about_us/ history.html> (June 27, 2007).

6. Interview with Holli Litwiller, guardian ad litem, May 2007.

7. "Tool Kit to End Violence Against Women," National Advisory Council on Violence Against Women and the Violence Against Women Office, n.d., <http://toolkit.ncjrs.org/files/fullchapter12.pdf> (January 28, 2008).

8. Interview with Ron Hitchcock, Marriage and Family Life Pastor, Vineyard Church of Columbus, Ohio, May 2007.

9. Hon. Laurence D. Kay (Ret.), "An Open Letter to the California Judiciary: Administration of Justice in Domestic Violence Cases,"

p. 166, 2005, <www.courtinfo.ca.gov/programs/cfcc/pdffiles/11_ Kay.pdf> (January 2015).

10. Ibid., pp. 165, 166

abuse—A way in which one person exerts power and control over another person to try to get a desired result. It can include physical abuse, emotional abuse, verbal abuse, sexual abuse, or a combination of these. Abuse is not a one-time act; there is a pattern to the behavior. It is both repeated and sustained.

bullying—A method of intimidating another person using threats and humiliation and sometimes physical force, such as pushing or shoving.

commercial sexual exploitation of children (CSEC)—A form of sexual abuse that involves a cash payment to the child or a third person. The child is treated as a commercial object and a sexual object. It can involve prostitution, pornography, and the sale of children for sexual purposes.

cutting—A form of self-injury, self-harm, or self-abuse in which people slice their skin with an object.

cyberabuse (also called cyberbullying or cyberstalking)— A type of abuse that involves online harassment and can include sending threatening e-mails or instant messages, posting offensive comments online, sending harassing text messages via cellular phones, threatening or intimidating someone through electronic text, borrowing someone's screen name and pretending to be them online, forwarding private pictures and videos to others, etc.

cycle of abuse—The repeating pattern of abuse that involves three, or sometimes four, phases. These phases include the tension-building phase, the incident phase, the make-up phase, and the calm phase. Understanding the cycle is an important tool in helping to assess the danger of an abusive situation.

discipline—A form of correction used by parents to address poor behavior or choices in their children. It is a form of teaching that helps children learn what is right and what is wrong.

domestic violence—A type of abuse between two intimate partners, such as a husband and wife or a boyfriend and girlfriend, that involves physical abuse, sexual assault, and/or the threat of physical abuse or sexual assault.

emotional abuse—The most subtle form of abuse including verbal attacks, withholding emotional support and approval, withholding money, etc.

exploitation—Using another person for selfish purposes that are usually sexual in nature (see commercial sexual exploitation of children—CSEC).

Family to Family model—A national model for organizations dealing with abuse. The model has four basic beliefs including a child's safety is the top concern, children belong in families, families need strong communities, and child welfare systems need to partner with the community and with others.

guardian ad litem—A volunteer appointed by a judge to represent the interests of an abused or neglected child in court.

incest—Sexual abuse and/or rape of a young person by an immediate family member or someone living in their home.

molestation—A form of sexual abuse that can involve physical contact or interactions that are sexual in nature, such as exposing an adult's private parts, making a child view pornography, etc. Typically the abuser is older than the victim and in a position of power or authority.

neglect—Failure to provide proper care for another person, including food, housing, clothing, medical care, supervision, and emotional support.

physical abuse—A form of abuse that leaves marks, inflicts pain, or causes injury. It can include hitting, pushing, shoving, slapping, shaking, pinching, biting, restraining, grabbing, choking, beating, burning, whipping, kicking, etc.

prejudicial bullying—Bullying based on the prejudices young people have toward people of different races, religions, and sexual orientations.

punishment—An unhealthy and sometimes abusive form of correction that is harmful in some way, such as slapping, beating, or name-calling.

rape—Sometimes called sexual assault; it involves unwanted sex that is forced either physically or through the threat of force.

relational aggression—Sometimes called emotional bullying; it involves social manipulation where young people try to hurt their peers or sabotage their social standing.

resiliency—The ability to cope and even thrive after negative experiences such as abuse.

restraining order—Sometimes called a protective order, this court order requires someone to stop abusing another person. It also may state that the person cannot see or contact the victim. These orders vary from state to state because each state defines abuse differently.

sexual abuse—Involves any type of sexual contact (physical, nonphysical, or violent in nature) between an adult and a child. It can also happen between an older child and younger child or between two teens.

sexual assault—It is sometimes called rape and involves unwanted sex that is forced either physically or through the threat of force.

sexual bullying—Repeated harmful and humiliating actions that target a person sexually. Examples include sexual name-calling (such as slut), crude comments, vulgar gestures, and sexual propositioning.

sexual harassment—Unwelcome sexual attention that is either physical or verbal in nature or a combination of both. It can occur at work, at school, and online.

stalking—Harassing or threatening behaviors that continually occur. These behaviors include following a person, appearing at the person's home, making harassing phone calls, leaving written messages, and vandalizing property. Stalking can also occur online and is called cyberstalking, cyberabuse, or cyberbullying. Many times stalking can lead to physical violence.

trafficking—Involves moving people from one place to another for the purpose of sex, slavery, or forced labor. It involves a series of events, including acquiring the people, moving them, and exploiting them. Sometimes force, drugs, or tricks are used to do this.

verbal abuse—A type of abuse used to define another person with words and name-calling. It is also used to define another person's thoughts, feelings, and motives.

For More Information

Break the Cycle National Headquarters
5200 W. Century Boulevard, Suite 300
Los Angeles, CA 90045
Helpline: 888-988-TEEN
(310) 286-3383
breakthecycle.org

Child Welfare Information Gateway
Children's Bureau/ACYF
1250 Maryland Avenue SW
Eighth Floor
Washington, D.C. 20024
(800) 394-3366
childwelfare.gov

National Center for Victims of Crime
2000 M Street NW, Suite 480
Washington, D.C. 20036
(202) 467-8700
victimsofcrime.org

National Center on Domestic and Sexual Violence
4612 Shoal Creek Boulevard
Austin, TX 78756
(512) 407-9020
ncdsv.org

National Coalition Against Domestic Violence
1120 Lincoln Street, Suite 1603
Denver, CO 80203
(303) 839-1852
ncadv.org

The National Crime Prevention Council

1000 Connecticut Avenue NW, 13th Floor

Washington, D.C. 20036

(202) 466-6272

ncpc.org

National Criminal Justice Reference Service

P.O. Box 6000

Rockville, MD 20849-6000

(800) 851-3420

ncjrs.gov

National Domestic Violence Hotline

1-800-799-SAFE (7233)

thehotline.org

National Network to End Domestic Violence

1400 16th St NW, Suite 330

Washington, DC 20036

(202) 543-5566

nnedv.org/

National Teen Dating Abuse Helpline

(866) 331-9474

(866) 331-8453

loveisrespect.org

OneVOICE Enterprises

iamonevoice.org

Prevent Child Abuse America

500 N. Michigan Avenue

Suite 200

Chicago, IL 60611

(312) 663-3520

preventchildabuse.org

Rape, Abuse & Incest National Network

2000 L Street NW, Suite 406
Washington, DC 20036
(800) 656-HOPE (4673) extension 3
rainn.org

U.S. Department of Justice, Office on Violence Against Women

800 K Street NW, Suite 920
Washington, D.C. 20530
(202) 307-6026
justice.gov/ovw

VAWnet

6400 Flank Drive, Suite 1300
Harrisburg, PA 17112-2778
(800) 537-2238
vawnet.org

Web Sites

loveisrespect.org

Love Is Respect promotes healthy relationships.

ohl.rainn.org/online

The Rape, Abuse & Incest National Network (RAINN) Online Hotline will give you immediate help anonymously.

Further Reading

Brown, Tracy. *Cyberbullying: Online Safety*. New York: Rosen Classroom, 2013.

Culp, Jennifer. *I Have Been Sexually Abused. Now What?* New York: Rosen Publishing Group, 2015.

Hall, Megan Kelly. *Dear Bully: Seventy Authors Tell Their Story*. New York: HarperTeen, 2011.

Henneberg, Susan. *I Have Been Raped. Now What?* New York: Rosen Publishing Group, 2015.

Kenney, Karen Latchana. *Domestic Violence (Essential Issues)*. Edina, Minn.: Abdo Group, 2011.

Lily, Henrietta M. *Teen Dating Violence*. New York: Rosen Publishing Group, 2011.

Piehl, Norah. *Date Rape (Issues that Concern You)*. Detroit, Mich.: Greenhaven Press, 2012.

Ryan, Peter. *Online Bullying*. New York: Rosen Publishing Group, 2011.

Index

A

academic issues, 63
alcohol and drugs, 16, 21, 32, 45, 58–59, 64–65, 67, 69, 71, 76, 80
Amanda, 57–59
American Academy of Child and Adolescent Psychiatry, 27
anorexia, 58, 64
A Safe Place, 67

B

batterer intervention program, 82, 87, 89–90
Becker, Gavin de, 84
Belinda, 25
binge eating, 58, 64–65
Bromley, Nicole Braddock, 11, 21, 29, 31, 52–53, 81, 92
bulimia, 64
bullying, 14, 46, 48–49

C

calm phase, 17, 19
Carrie, 77-78
Center for Child and Family Advocacy, 98
Charron, Paul R., 39
child abuse, 24, 65, 70-71, 73, 82-83, 93
Child Abuse Protection Act of 1990, 83
child protective services, 25, 72, 73
Child Welfare League of America, 56
Christy, 32
Claiborne, Liz, 39
commercial sexual exploitation of children (CSEC), 16
Council on Sexual Assault and Domestic Violence, 43
court-appointed special advocates (CASA), 83, 99. *See also* guardian ad litem.
Crompton, Jenny, 37-38, 44
Crompton, Vicki, 38, 43
Cut It Out, 74
cyberabuse (cyberstalking, cyberbullying), 14, 16, 49, 88
cycle of abuse, 20, 67, 68

D

dating violence, 38, 44, 65, 84
depression, 59, 61, 63, 65
discipline, 24
domestic violence (domestic abuse and intimate partner violence), 10, 32-34, 36, 39, 43-44, 67, 69, 73, 82, 84, 93, 95, 98, 100

E

eating disorders, 58, 63-65

Eckhardt, Christopher, 90, 92
emotional abuse, 8, 13-14, 20, 24, 61
Evans, Patricia, 13, 61
exploitation, 14, 16, 55, 70, 82. *See also* trafficking.

F
Facebook, 48, 50
FaceTime, 14
Family to Family model, 98
fear, 17, 27, 31, 33-34, 36-37, 44-45, 60-61, 64, 74, 84, 87-88

G
gangs, 56, 71-72
grooming, 20, 31
guardian ad litem, 83, 99

H
harassment (sexual harassment), 12, 14, 16, 53, 55, 88
Hitchcock, Ron, 100, 102
Holly, 39-40

I
incest, 12, 30, 82, 92
incident phase, 17, 19
Instagram, 49-50
Internet, 10, 14, 49, 50, 88
Interstate Stalking Act, 88

K
Katie, 7-9
Kay, Laurence D., 102

L
Litwiller, Holli, 99

M
make-up phase, 17, 19
Miranda, 46, 48
molestation, 12, 31, 52
Murray, Jill, 83-84

N
neglect, 14, 61, 65, 70-71, 73, 82-83, 99

O
One Love Foundation, 9
OneVOICE Enterprises, 11, 30
order of protection, 86. *See also* restraining order.

P
Paige, 23-25
Penn State, 52
Perry, Bruce, 61
physical abuse, 9, 10, 12, 14, 25, 27, 32, 36, 43, 45, 64, 71, 82, 89, 93
pornography, 12, 16, 20-21, 27, 31, 82
post-traumatic stress disorder (PTSD), 58, 60
power and control, 10-12, 19-21, 32, 38, 41, 43, 45-46, 53, 77, 84, 86, 90
prejudicial bullying, 14
prostitution, 16, 55-56, 59, 65
punishment, 23-25, 31, 65, 69, 73, 92

R

rape, 8-9, 12, 20, 39-41, 58-59, 64, 82, 87-88. *See also* sexual assault.
rape shield laws, 87
relational aggression, 14
resiliency, 67-68
restraining order, 86-88

S

Sandusky, Jerry, 52
Saving Beauty from the Beast, 38
self-injury (cutting, self-abuse, and self-harm), 25, 27, 48
sex offender (sexual predator), 20, 50, 52-53, 55, 92
sexual abuse, 9-12, 14, 16-17, 20-21, 24, 27, 29-32, 36, 52, 53, 64-65, 71, 73, 80, 82, 89-90, 92-93
sexual assault, 12, 20, 39-41, 87, 92-93
sexual bullying, 14
sexual offender treatment program, 89-90, 92
Smith, Mark, 37, 38
spanking, 23, 24
stalking, 14, 16, 38, 80, 87-88
suicide, 25, 28, 48, 59, 63, 65
symptoms of abuse, 34, 59

T

Teenage Research Unlimited, 38
teen pregnancy, 45, 59, 64, 65
tension-building phase, 16-17

Thurman, Tracey, 95
time span, 20
trafficking, 14, 16, 55, 82, 88
Twitter, 50, 52

U

Urban, Beth, 63, 67, 72, 93, 96, 98
US Department of Justice, 55, 56
US Equal Employment Opportunity Commission (EEOC), 53

V

verbal abuse, 9, 13-14, 17, 20, 24-25, 32, 43, 61, 73, 89, 100, 102
Violence Against Women Act, 95

W

warning signs, 45, 74

Y

YouTube, 49-50